On Broken Pieces

Dr. Carolyn C. Carlisle

DEDICATION

This book is dedicated to a brand new "ME". This book is also dedicated to those men and women living on broken pieces of the residual aftereffects of domestic violence: guilt, shame, anger, denial, bitterness, grief, low self-esteem, eating disorders, insomnia, fear, and post-traumatic stress disorders, to name a few. I wrote this book to help others by empowering, encouraging, inspiring and uplifting survivors of domestic violence to let them know that broken pieces can be made whole again. I wrote this book to help fuel someone else into healing and wholeness by breaking the silence of what happened to you and sharing your story. I wrote this book to inspire survivors of domestic violence to take steps in their own healing using their own voices. The aftereffects of domestic violence thrive easily in isolation but loses its power when people come together to share their common experiences. The truth will set you free. My journey to heal has been based on a very simple truth: I was broken. I was living on broken pieces. I had to acknowledge my truth to myself and speak the truth to become free. It is a process; however, with support everyone can achieve it.

PREFACE

There is a plethora of aftereffects of surviving domestic violence: anger, denial, grief, low self-esteem, guilt, shame, fear, etc., just to name a few. This literary work will focus mainly on guilt and shame.

On Broken Pieces was birthed as a result of my surviving domestic violence and my quest to bring healing, hope, and wholeness to those harboring the aftereffects as a result of surviving sexual and domestic violence. Scholarly research on the aftereffects of guilt and shame as it relates to surviving domestic violence and the role of the church was conducted in my doctoral studies while matriculating at United Theological Seminary in Dayton, Ohio. In the *Biblical and Ethical Engagement for Social and Moral Imperatives Cohort* group we were challenged to develop new paradigms in ministry that would address social and moral dilemmas people are challenged with today. Addressing domestic violence in the local church and providing support ministries for survivors of domestic violence is certainly a new paradigm for many. Domestic violence is an epidemic worldwide and affects persons of all genders, ethnicities, cultures, and economic statuses in every church denomination. And yet, many of our pastors and church leaders are silent on the issue. There is no healing in silence!

I understand, from my own case, that even after ending the abusive relationship, residual guilt and shame have to be addressed. Left unaddressed, guilt and shame will have a detrimental effect on the survivor of domestic violence and continued victimization is likely to occur. Positing from my own healing of guilt and shame associated with domestic violence, as well as drinking from the well of my experiences, this book adds my voice to the conversation of healing the aftereffects of guilt and shame associated with domestic violence. May God's grace abound in the local church, as we become that bridge that carries love and acceptance to survivors of domestic violence who are suffering with the aftereffects of guilt and shame.

Today I choose to shine a light in the place of darkness.

CONTENTS

Acknowledgments

Introduction

1   Broken   14

2   Addressing Brokenness   20

3   The Undergirding   32

4   The Approach   48

5   Field Experience   50

6   Reflections   56

   Appendices   61

   Bibliography   72

ACKNOWLEDGMENTS

I am so grateful to those persons who inspired and supported me in the writing of this book.

Children are a blessing from The Lord. My two PK's (Preacher Kids): Jason Marquis Carlisle and Jasmine Jacari' Carlisle are truly blessings. Thank you for being uniquely you. Thank you, Jason, for speaking words of wisdom, at a young age, that inspired me to seek help and encouraging me to "speak out" against domestic violence. The timing of articulating your wisdom was life changing. This has been a long and arduous journey and you have been right by my side. Thank you, Jasmine, for helping me to see that I am fearfully and wonderfully made.

Dr. Vanessee J. Burns, Lead Pastor of Christian Chapel Temple of Faith, Dallas, Texas. Thank you for mentorship, friendship and your **strong** encouragement for me being who God called me to be. Thank you for inspiring me.

To my siblings, Marandra Rivers and Jacquelyn Clark, thank you for loving me in all my seasons. Thank you, Jacquelyn, for sheltering me in the times of storm.

To Dr. Adrian C. Evans, thank you for the enthusiastic support, passionate push, editing, and encouragement. Thank you for being you: always willing to help others and give graciously of yourself. I am so appreciative to be one of the recipients.

To Ms. Leslie Hughes thank you for utilizing your gift of words to ensure that my writing was clear. Thank you for believing that my writing is phenomenal, powerful, necessary and life changing. Thank you for boosting my confidence. I believe that now too!

To all of you, who have supported, encouraged, assisted and help lift me out of the pain of living on broken pieces, thank you.

INTRODUCTION

Recently, a series of public service announcements have aired with celebrities and professional football players articulating their commitment to advocating against domestic violence. In these announcements, they have expressed that they will no longer accept excuses for domestic violence, while simultaneously no longer provide excuses for not getting involved. These recent public service announcements resonated in my inner being, immediately prompting my thought, "If only pastors would also make a commitment to addressing domestic violence in the local church and provide support ministries for survivors of domestic violence, the impact would be profound." As a pastor, I joined the celebrities and professional football players in their denouncing of domestic violence and vowed to bring awareness into the church.

Domestic violence is an epidemic worldwide and affects persons of all genders, ethnicities, cultures, and economic statuses in every church denomination. And yet, many of our pastors are silent on the issue. "Churches should be talking about abuse because statistically some of our men are abusing women,"[1] and it is time for pastors to finally shatter the silence on domestic violence. "The community of faith must deal with domestic violence because it has penetrated our families, our neighborhoods, our community, our churches and our world."[2] It is the church's duty to confront the issue, showing love and compassion for those who are being abused, while simultaneously holding perpetrators accountable. Consequently, the church is called to address all immorality and evil not just selective issues. "Domestic violence is not only a crime against humanity; it is a sin against God...Yet a greater crime exists. It is the crime of apathy and silence."[3] There is urgency in pastors establishing ministries within the local church to address domestic violence and create ways to help survivors of domestic violence because God does not condone domestic violence. Yet, when women leave an abusive relationship, the church is usually not the place where help is readily available. Pastors must act now!

One of the most crucial times for survivors of domestic violence is when they leave an abusive relationship. Women survivors of domestic violence often leave

---

[1] Ron Clark, *Setting the Captives Free: a Christian Theology for Domestic Violence* (Eugene, OR: Cascade Books, 2005), xx.

[2] Clark, xxi.

[3] Ibid., xxi.

abusive relationships bruised, emotionally scarred and overwhelmed with guilt and shame. Rarely are there support ministries within the local church to address the aftereffects of guilt and shame, the foci of this project. Yet, in the Digital Video Disc, *Speaking of Faith: Domestic Violence Programs and the African American Church*, church leaders show how domestic violence ministries can and should be incorporated in church. This project purports that the role of the church is to provide support ministry for domestic violence survivors. "A Christian community is therefore a healing community, not because wounds are cured and pains are alleviated, but because wounds and pains become openings or occasions for a new vision."[4] The new vision is for churches to actively take the lead in developing ministries within the church to support women survivors of domestic violence. Although a few churches have embraced this new vision, other churches must act now!

As a survivor of domestic violence, in Chapter One, I share how my own experiences have driven urgency for the need of churches to address the aftereffects of guilt and shame. I understand that left unaddressed, guilt and shame will have a detrimental effect on survivors of domestic violence. I share my experience of being abused while still assembling weekly in a church that was silent on the issue of domestic violence. Sermons, literature, or the mention of domestic violence was not a part of my faith community. Thus, my healing did not come from a caring church community but occurred in peer focus group settings where I was able to dialog and share my story with other survivors of domestic violence. Consequently, I believe that the church is an appropriate place where ministries for survivors of domestic violence desperately need to be birthed. The model takes as its point of departure, storytelling as a means of dialoging, reframing, and reshaping lives for survivors of domestic violence.

Chapter Two investigates how offering space for female domestic violence survivors to meet in peer focus group settings and share their stories about the aftereffects of guilt and shame contributes positively to better self-esteem and aids in initiating healing. Working with women in the local church setting, the ministry project will reveal how the church can serve as an important role in shattering the silence on domestic violence and could be a place for addressing the aftereffects of guilt and shame associated with surviving domestic violence. This chapter will show that the failure to address these issues of guilt and shame for survivors of domestic violence is an injustice. Social justice is supposed to be the main focus of the church. The church must regain its focus of being a place for providing liberation. Most importantly, research shows that healing of guilt and shame cannot be accomplished in isolation.

Chapter Three provides the biblical, historical and theological foundations for

---

[4] Henri J. M. Nouwen, *The Wounded Healer: Ministry in Contemporary Society* (New York: Image Books, 1979), 100.

this work. Scripture from the Old Testament will be analyzed to show the aftereffects of guilt and shame experienced by a female domestic violence survivor, the effects that domestic violence has on the family, and what happens to the abused when the faith community fails to validate a victim's worth and thus silence her voice. Scripture from the New Testament will be analyzed to show that our ministry focus must be on enacting liberation. Historically, domestic violence can be traced backed to biblical times where women were seen as the property of a man. Research will show how patriarchy contributed to men exhibiting power and control over women, which also are dominant factors in domestic violence. We will look through the lenses of liberation, feminist and womanist theologies as tools for liberating women survivors of domestic violence. Liberation theology teaches about empowering from oppression. The failure of addressing the aftereffects of guilt and shame is an injustice; therefore, we must correct it and do justice. Elizabeth Cady Stanton, a feminist, will show the equality of the sexes; therefore, women are made equal to men and thus have the same power. Womanist theology through the voices of Jacquelyn Grant, Delores Williams, and Alice Walker will speak to the experience of African American Women and call for specific ways of enacting healing. While we have acknowledged that domestic violence and its aftereffects of guilt and shame know no boundary lines when it comes to factors such as ethnicity or culture, our focus for this project is African American women.

Chapter Four provides the hypothesis and model for this project. Survivors of domestic violence can be supported in the local church and resourced for conquering the emotions of guilt and shame. As a solution, a design model for creating space, in the local church, conducive to sharing the aftereffects of guilt and shame was accomplished. The design was built to include surveys, observations, and focus groups. Measurement occurred through pre-and posttest continuum, depicting the degree of guilt and shame exhibited at the onset of the focus group versus the degree of guilt and shame by participants after having gone through six sessions. I chose this model because I believe that pastors and church leaders must address the issues that are relevant to the people they serve. I believe, just as Dr. Edward Smith Davis believes when he posits that "in order to serve people, we must hear them."[5] The goal of the model was to hear the voices of women who survived domestic violence yet still harbored feelings of guilt and shame, for members of the peer focus group to have named guilt and shame as one of the aftereffects of domestic violence, work through sharing their stories to embark upon the beginning of healing of those emotions, and gain a boost in their self-esteem while peeling off layers of guilt and shame.

---

[5] Edward Smith Davis, "Ethical and Biblical Engagement for Social and Moral Imperatives: The Trials and Joys, the Ins and Outs of Being a Conference Minister with its Diversity" (lecture, Southern Conference of the United Church of Christ Headquarters, Burlington, NC, December 9, 2014).

Chapter Five provides the field experience developed through collaborative effort of Context and Professional Associates. Five African American women survivors of domestic violence shared through storytelling their stories of surviving domestic violence and aftereffects of living with guilt and shame as they journeyed through six sessions of group. A focus was provided for each of the six sessions. Session One's focus was introduction of the project and model; Session Two's focus was defining and working through the aftereffects of guilt; Session Three's focus was defining and working through the aftereffects of shame; Session Four's focus was sharing of stories; Session Five's focus was self-esteem and Session Six's focus was celebration. During the field experience, guilt was released and shame lessened. Secrets were exposed as women articulated for the first time some of their experiences and how it affected them. Women who previously were unable to look at pictures or view themselves in the mirror because of feeling ugly, flawed, and unimportant were able to complete two mirror exercises and repeat their own positive affirmations to themselves. Women participated in a releasing ritual whereby they were able to write all the negative, blameful accusations experienced that they wanted to release on strips of paper, gather outside and burn.

Chapter Six covers a summary and reflects on the importance of the church pastors taking the lead in providing support services in their churches for parishioners who are experiencing the aftereffects of guilt and shame associated with domestic violence. If healing is to be initiated and survivors transformed from victims to survivors to conquerors, then women must be validated and their voices must be heard – in the local church. The project was a success but there were some lessons learned. The consistency of conducting the group went well. Women survivors who were ready to do the work necessary for healing participated during the duration of the project. Those women were able to articulate through voice their cries that had been silenced for so long. Guilt and shame were named as an aftereffect by all survivors of domestic violence. Sadly, two of the participants did not complete the entire six sessions and the Mary Kay Consultant did not honor her commitment in providing facials to the participants. I suggest in Chapter Six some alternative ways of fine-tuning the model.

During a recent conversation over dinner with one of my colleagues, Rev. Lavisha Williams, my initial position of pastors becoming involved in advocating against domestic violence became much clearer. Rev. Williams was sharing about an upcoming preaching engagement she had where Jonah 1 would be used as her pericope. She shared how God had laid on her heart the question in Jonah 1:6, "How can you sleep at such a time as this? God had called Jonah to go to Nineveh and cry out against the wickedness that was going on in the city. Jonah was disobedient, fled from the Lord and went in the opposite direction. Jonah paid his fare, boarded a ship and went down to the bottom deck and went to sleep. God caused a fierce storm at sea and the ship was in danger of being broken up. The sailors were terrified. The sailors were above on deck doing everything possible to lighten the load of the ship, fighting the storm and fighting for their lives. Imagine the scene on deck, high winds, roaring waves, terrified sailors who were screaming directions, throwing the attached anchor overboard to help stabilize the ship. The sailors were also sailing with cargo. Sailing with cargo is a money-making enterprise and you do not want to anger the ship's owner by having thrown over what amounts to his money; however, as a last resort, the sailors threw over the cargo. While all of this is going on above, Jonah is on the bottom deck fast asleep. The captain goes below and awakes Jonah. The captain asks how can you sleep at a time like this?

My spirit leaped. This question resonated so with me and the issue of churches failing to address the prevalent issue of domestic violence. How can you sleep pastors at a time like this when boys and men daily are speaking out about being molested for years by pastors, church leaders and priests? How can you sleep pastors at a time like this when daily women are coming forth speaking out about years of abuse and sexual misconduct behaviors by the likes of Bill Cosby, Tavis Smiley, Matt Lauer, Russell Simmons, Harvey Weinstein, John Conyers, Jr., Roy Moore, Al Franken, George H.W. Bush, James Franco, Morgan Spurlock, Marshall Faulk, Ike Taylor, Heath Evans, Mario Batali, Steven Segal, and the list goes on and on? How can you sleep pastors when some man, woman, boy or girl in your congregation is battered and there are no support ministries available at your church to walk side them to healing and wholeness? How can you sleep pastors when perpetrators are on your official boards and are officers in your church and you know of their behavior; yet you are silent? How can you sleep pastors when pastors themselves are perpetrators of violence and never seek help or is held accountable? How can you sleep at such a time as this? I choose not to sleep!

1 BROKEN

Outgoing, vivacious, popular and jovial described me yet none of these positive attributes could protect me from the disheartening life experiences that I would encounter; experiences stained with rejection, abandonment, brokenness, guilt and shame. Broken, cracked, shattered and not together. Normally when things I owned were broken, cracked, shattered and just not together, I would throw them away. But this time, what was broken, cracked, shattered and just not together was ME! How could I possibly throw myself away?

I was broken. Marriage was not what I visualized. Six months after being married, physical abuse was occurring to me. This was still supposed to literally be my honeymoon! Surely, honeymoons lasted more than six months. Or did they? For me, it did not.

The first occurrence of abuse happened while living in an apartment complex. My husband was spending a great deal of time downstairs with a single, Caucasian female and her children. When I questioned him about it, he approached me with a knife. Survival instincts surfaced and I immediately ran out of the apartment. One of my male friends saw me running and tried to help me escape by opening the passenger door of his car but to no avail. My husband pulled me from the car and roughly escorted me back to the apartment. Verbal and physical abuse continued that night. I was broken.

The vicious cycle of abuse would continue long afterwards: open-hand slaps, verbal abuse, name calling, accusations, abusive anger, threats of violence and futuristic threats of violence were merely just some of the violence that I endured. I went through the vicious cycle of honeymoon, tension, and violence. My life appeared to be on a merry-go-round. A year later, I birthed my son, Jason; yet, the cycle of abuse continued.

During the two-year duration of abuse, I still attended church weekly for Bible Study and Sunday Worship. I wore a façade and attended services pretending that everything was fine. I was broken. Life was miserable; however, attending church and working were my only releases. Sadly, there were other women within our church who were also experiencing domestic violence and suffering in their own silence. We all assembled weekly, singing and praying about a loving God, but no one wanted to address the elephant in the sanctuary. Rod Buxton explained the phenomenon most accurately when stating, "The church is a place to be involved with loving, caring, and functional people. The problem is that these people are often found to be so 'functional' they will not even talk about domestic violence; let alone actually admit that they could be experiencing abuse from a spouse."[6]

I, along with other women, suffered silently in church. Though I was a functional member of the church, teaching Women's Sunday school class, serving as President of the Matron's Society, an Usher and Youth Director, I contributed to the elephant in the sanctuary by remaining silent and refusing to acknowledge my abuse. Marla F. Frederick's work on southern black women and their everyday struggles of faith speak volume of my broken situation in her simple title, *Between Sundays*. Frederick writes, "in spite of the problems within the church, women not only remain members they worship, participate, teach Sunday school, usher on the Usher's Board, give their tithe, form community outreaches, and in a large sense undergird the entire operation of the church."[7] My abuse rarely occurred on Sundays but it was between Sundays that my life was a living hell. In, *Between Sundays*, Fredericks speaks to my past brokenness where she writes, "On Sundays we, as Christian believers, go to church, and we find grace that heals the broken places, hope to enter the coming week, and strength to meet its challenges. Sunday is where we make sense of it all. Monday, Tuesday, Wednesday, Thursday, Friday and Saturday all come together on Sunday."[8] Frederick described my experience precisely – Sundays somehow gave me hope that there could be better possibilities for the remainder of the week.

Hope can come in various ways. Frederick states, "Whether from the preaching of the word, the inspiration of the choir, or the testimony of the saints, on Sunday opportunities are found and answers are discovered."[9] Music has always been a vital part of my being: so much of my inspiration came from the choir, and music was where I found my hope. I carried with me the lyrics to a song the choir sung, entitled "There's a brighter day ahead."

Unfortunately, my hopeful inspiration certainly did not come from the preaching of the Word on domestic violence because I never once heard a sermon preached on the subject while I was attending church. There were no workshops hosted or domestic violence pamphlets in the foyer or women's restroom at the church. It seems as if the leaders believed that if domestic violence were never

---

[6] Rod Buxton, "Domestic violence in the church: 'there is an elephant in the sanctuary and no-one is talking about it' the results of a Manitoba survey." *Didaskalia (Otterburne, Man.)* 12, no. 1:51-75. *ATLA Religion Database with ATLASerials, EBSCOhost* (accessed May 2, 2014), 53.

[7] Marla F. Frederick, *Between Sundays: Black Women and Everyday Struggle of Faith* (Berkeley, CA: University of California Press, 2003), 4.

[8] Ibid, 210.

[9] Ibid., 210.

mentioned in church, it would go away. Al Miles in, *Domestic Violence: What Every Pastor Needs to Know*, documents that "Clergy people have often not been helpful in dealing with the problem of domestic violence. While many women affirm the overall value of their religious faith, few say that spiritual leaders have supported their struggle to leave an abusive situation. In fact, several women have told me that their pastors' responses have stifled their healing process."[10] For me, the church's silence on the issue of domestic violence meant that domestic violence was condoned. This added more confusion to my state of being – my brokenness. There were times that I wanted to scream, "I am being abused!" Yet, I continued to assemble weekly with a community of believers of various degrees – some abused and some perpetrators of the violence themselves.

I was living on eggshells. I tried to tread lightly – so I thought! I was living in a state of not knowing what to expect when I arrived home or what disposition my husband would possess when he arrived home. Living like this was stressful. It was now nearing the end of year two and things had gotten progressively worse. Marriage was certainly not what I had envisioned. I sought relief from being battered by leaving on several occasions but somehow managed to always return. R. Emerson Dobash and Russell P. Dobash, well known for their research on abused women, states, "far from helplessly remaining with violent men, women engage in an active process we refer to as 'staying, leaving, and returning'."[11] In essence, according to Dobash and Dobash, women hope that temporary departure from the home will assist with the perpetrator's reform.

> Women make active and conscious decisions based on their changing circumstances: they leave for short periods in order to escape the violence and to emphasize their disaffection in the hope that this will stop the violence. In the beginning, they are generally not attempting to end the relationship, but are negotiating to reestablish the relationship on a non-violent basis.[12]

I, along with so many others that I personally know, have performed the staying, leaving, and returning routine. Sometimes my departure lasted a day, sometimes a week, sometimes much longer; however, in the end I always returned.

I wanted so badly to honor my marriage vows that I remained in this volatile marriage with a substance abuser and perpetrator of violence for two years enduring

---

[10] Al Miles, *Domestic Violence: What Every Pastor Needs to Know* (Minneapolis, MN: Fortress Press, 2000), 23.

[11] R. Emerald Dobash and Russell P. Dobash. *Women, Violence & Social Change* (New York, NY: Routledge, 1994), 231.

[12] Ibid., 231.

abuse from seven months after marriage until the end. Fear gripped me – fearful of leaving permanently because of constant threats and fear for my life if I remained. I found that dissolving this marriage was difficult. "Breaking up with an abuser can be very hard to do. In fact, leaving a non-abusive partner is generally easier, contrary to what many people believe," writes Lundy Bancroft in *Why Does He Do That?*[13] I found this to be true.

The breakup was painful and dangerous. I was truly fearful of the outcome. So, fearful that I found a two-bedroom apartment in the city that was income based and moved out without my husband knowledge. Small city, small town! My husband somehow found out where I had moved. When he discovered my new living arrangement, he came to the apartment complex and climbed up into the outside ceiling tiles above my front door, recovering the tiles as to not expose his presence and waited until I arrived home. On this particular day, one of my cousins was with my son and I as we arrived home. Upon reaching the front door, my husband uncovered the ceiling tiles, jumped down and began beating me. My child watched, my cousin ran and called the police. My husband left before the police arrive however not before abusing me physically. This became one of the many long nights.

The next day while at work, my husband approached me and created a disturbing scene. He came and approached me trying to coerce me to be in conversation with him. By now, I had realized that I could not conduct a rational conversation with an abusive husband. When I refused to converse with him, he became angry. One of my co-workers witnessed the incident and called security. Security escorted him off the premises. That same week, he moved to Birmingham, Alabama, leaving our previously leased apartment, furniture, clothes and all of his possessions. Several months later he was incarcerated again. For me, however, my embedded theology of taking the vows "till death do us part" literally, had almost cost me my life.

I petitioned the Court for a divorce. It was difficult after the divorce. I now had a small baby boy and was overwhelmed with the duties of being a single mother. I was broken. I was no longer being abused; nevertheless, I had many more challenges to overcome emotionally. I experienced a plethora of emotions: anger, denial, grief, low self-esteem, guilt and shame; however, guilt and shame overwhelmingly followed me. "Shame and guilt could be called the interpersonal emotions, because both tell us there is something wrong between us and the rest of the world. Both ask us to look at ourselves carefully and to make changes in our

---

[13] Lundy Bancroft, *Why Does He Do That? Inside the Minds of Angry and Controlling Men,* Reprint ed. (New York, NY: Berkley Books, 2001), 213.

lives."[14]

I was literally wallowing in guilt and shame. I was divorced but where would I go from here? Even though my ex-husband and I were miles away from each other, I still felt extremely guilty and shameful about the abuse. I had never planned on being a single parent. Paralyzing questions were constantly on my mind. *What was I to tell my son about his father? Would my son have a positive male role model in his life? Who was going to teach him how to mow the lawn or drive a car? Would I ever trust another man and enter unto a loving, monogamous relationship?* I had more questions than answers. I still attended a church that did not address the issue of domestic violence and was not a resource for helping me cope with my issues of guilt and shame.

For the next six years, I worked and raise my son as a single parent, never entering into an intimate relationship with another man. I dated other men casually but nothing serious. There was a void in my life. Even after the way my first marriage ended, I still made frequent contact with my ex-husband who was incarcerated through letter writing and occasional visits. By year seven, after being divorce, my ex-husband and I were making plans to remarry. I believed that there was a change in him and since I had not established a relationship with another man, I entertained the idea of remarrying. The idea became a reality. I made elaborate plans in the remarrying process. I was going to have the church wedding ceremony that I had never had previously. I went all out in preparation for this wedding, sparing no expense.

We remarried. For three years of this second marriage, everything was wonderful. My husband had obtained a job, joined Alcoholics Anonymous Program, was attending his meetings regularly and had made a personal commitment to Jesus Christ. Our second child, Jasmine, was born and life was good. My guilt and shame was masked.

By year four, I noticed some inconsistencies in my husband's behavior and the people with whom he had begun to associate. Very soon thereafter, he returned to using alcohol and drugs, and now had even added extramarital affairs to that equation. While all of this was going on (abuse, infidelity, experiencing guilt, shame, anger, and denial), I found temporary satisfaction in shopping. I took the cliché "shop until you drop" to a new level. It became "shop until you max out your credit cards". And that is what I did.

By the end of year four, the abuse had also reemerged. Having never addressed the guilt and shame from the previous marriage and now experiencing abuse again, my degrees of guilt and shame increased. The brutal cycle of abuse intensified. Suffering abuse again was *déjà vu*. I had already experienced domestic violence from this same man before and yet; here I was again being abused. Twelve years earlier, God had allowed me to escape a domestically violent marriage yet I had returned to

---

[14] Ronald Potter-Efron and Patricia Potter-Efron, *Letting Go of Shame: Understanding How Shame Affects Your Life* (n/p: Hazelden, 1989), 3.

the same violent man from whom God had delivered me. I would have to go through a divorce process again in order to release myself from the domestic violence. I was still engulfed with guilt and shame. Emma J. Justes, in *Please Don't Tell*, articulated my plot at this stage of my life when she wrote, "when a person has been the victim of abuse perpetrated by another person, the victim feels shame about what has been done to them. What has been done in violence and violation causes victimized persons to experience themselves in a shameful way."[15]

Just as it had before, leaving this marriage for a second time almost cost me bodily harm. Severing ties occurred this time after an explosive night of verbal and physical abuse. When my husband left the house, I left with the kids, retreating to a safe place. On the next day, I returned to the house to get the car and take the children to school. Unbeknown to me, my husband was sitting in his truck in the back yard and when I took our daughter to school, he followed me. He tried to coerce me out of the vehicle. Other parents were dropping their children off at school while I remained inside the vehicle. This terrorism went on for about thirty minutes with his anger escalating. While this was occurring, our daughter was still in the vehicle with me, not fully comprehending what was happening. I finally attempted to get out of the car, somehow believing that if our daughter were beside me, he would not try to harm me. As I was trying to escort her into the school, my husband tore my tee shirt, ripping it badly and exposing my breasts, picked up a brick and stated that he was going to burst me in the head. Parents alerted school personnel and they in turn notified the police. Two police patrol cars entered the grounds of the school. One officer attended to my needs while the other officer talked with my husband. I asked the officer to escort me home to get some clothes, and I never returned to him or the house again until I was granted possession in the divorce. Double victimization, the appropriate name for my experience, did not help my feelings of guilt and shame. As a twice divorcee of a perpetrator of violence and a keeper of the secret that I had been abused, guilt and shame weighed heavily on my life and my decisions. Justes writes, "Keepers of secrets who have been abused or violated by others feel shame about their experience even though they did not cause the experience. When we are not at fault, we can still find ways to blame ourselves for what has been done to us. Telling what has happened; we fear, will confirm our role and solidify that shame."[16] I am sure that people suspected that I was being abused; however, I was ashamed to tell anyone about my abuse. I somehow believed that I would be labeled and carry a stigma if I allowed anyone to know that I was a victim of domestic violence. So instead, I suffered the guilt and shame silently and alone.

---

[15] Emma J. Justes, *Please Don't Tell: What to Do with the Secrets People Share* (Nashville, TN: Abingdon Press, 2014), 86.

[16] Justes, 86.

After leaving the house, I moved in temporarily with my sister while undergoing divorce proceedings. The divorce took almost six months before completion. I hired an attorney and filed an uncontested divorce, yet my husband refused to sign the papers. After realizing that I was not returning to this unstable marriage again, he reluctantly agreed to sign the papers. He was so accustomed to me following an autopilot cycle of leaving and returning that he was certain I would change my mind about divorcing him. I made a decision and this time I was sticking with it. Chip and Dan Heath, in *Decisive: How to Make Better Choices in Life and Work,* writes, "it's hard to interrupt these autopilot cycles, because, well, that's the whole point of autopilot. We don't think about what we're doing. We drift along in life, floating on the wake of past choices, and it's easy to forget that we have the ability to change direction."[17] The Heaths discuss a term called "tripwires" which are "signals that would snap us awake at exactly the right moment, compelling us to reconsider a decision or to make a new one."[18] A second marriage to the same abusive man with repeated abuse ignited a tripwire for me. I had three choices: divorce, jail or the grave. I chose divorce.

While I made the decision to end the marriage, I went through severe depression and limited activity. I was living on broken pieces. For the first three months after the divorce, my life consisted of going to work, coming home, and getting in bed. There were days I did not even want to get out of bed. My son, Jason, took care of his sister, Jasmine, for three months as I continued this depressive routine, completely overwhelmed with guilt and shame. I felt that God was silent and absent from my life. I felt rejected, abandoned, alone, guilty and shameful and my self-esteem was at an all-time low. I was convinced that I was the latest topic of discussion, so I disassociated from family and friends. I avoided people at all costs. I had more questions than answers, with paralyzing questions surfacing once again: *What am I going to do now? How will I make it? Can I afford to keep the house and take care of two children? How will this divorce affect the children? What will people think of me? How many people know that I was being abused? What did I do to cause the abuse?* These questions plagued my very existence. There were weekends when I pulled the cover over my head while in bed and simply cried. After three months of this depressive, guilt ridden and shameful behavior, Jason finally exclaimed, "Mom, you can't keep living like this. Dad has moved on with his life, and it is time that you accept that fact and move on too. You have two children to raise; now, snap out of it because we need you." There was nothing more impactful for me than the wisdom proclaimed by Jason, a child. Older people usually proclaim wise words, yet on this day, my son had provided me with wise advice that would literally change

---

[17] Chip Heath and Dan Heath, *Decisive: How to Make Better Choices in Life and Work* (New York, NY: Crown Business, 2013), 221.

[18] Ibid., 222.

my life, my behavior and my activities. Very, very, very, slowly, I regained my composure and began to live again. I underwent two years of psychological counseling. I had to look at myself and make some changes.

Domestic Violence is an issue that is unfortunately prevalent throughout the world. As stated earlier, I was not the only woman attending my local church who was abused. Moreover, the National Coalition against Domestic Violence posted on their website on September 11, 2014, the following abbreviated statement that substantiates that domestic violence is a prevalent problem globally.

> The National Coalition against Domestic Violence (NCADV) supports the National Football League (NFL) in its efforts to prevent domestic violence by suspending Ray Rice indefinitely. To finally be heard and have people understand the impact of domestic violence is encouraging. However, although this is a step in the right direction, NCADV recognizes that domestic violence does not live only on the football field. Violence against women spans worldwide. As a country, we have to look at domestic violence as a national problem – affecting women and families of all races, cultures, and income levels.[19]

Domestic Violence is not just a National Football League issue, domestic violence is a worldwide issue. It is an epidemic that can directly or indirectly touch all of us in one way or the other, whether it is through known and reported cases of family members, friends, or through our own case. My own case has driven urgency for this work, for I understand that even after ending the abusive relationship, residual guilt and shame still have to be addressed. Left unaddressed, guilt and shame will have a detrimental effect on the survivor of domestic violence and continued victimization is likely to occur.

---

[19] "Domestic Violence is Not Only an NFL Issue." National Coalition Against Domestic Violence (accessed September 11, 2014), http://www.ncadv.org//.

2 ADDRESSING BROKENNESS

One of the most crucial times for survivors of domestic violence occurs after the abusive relationship has ended. To be clear, I said, one of the most crucial times, not the most crucial time. Meg Kennedy Dugan and Roger R Hock states, "rarely is adequate consideration given to what many see as one of the most critical times for a survivor of an abusive relationship: the time after the survivor leaves."[20] The lack of ministry within the church to address the issues of guilt and shame associated with domestic violence hinders survivors of domestic violence from thriving, in their most precarious times of need. In, *Battered African American Women: A Study of Gender Entrapment*, Sharon Ellis Davis substantiates this when she posits, "Domestic Violence in African American communities is a crucial issue for the church. African American families are in crisis and it is imperative that African American churches deal with the issue of domestic violence in African American communities."[21]

This chapter investigates how offering space for domestic violence survivors to meet in peer groups and share their stories about the aftereffects of guilt and shame contributes positively to better self-esteem and aids in healing. As a form of pedagogy, survivors of domestic violence can learn to stop blaming and punishing themselves, two contributors to continued victimization. Several books from the social sciences ground this work and inform the need for addressing the aftereffects of guilt and shame of survivors of domestic violence.

In the Christian theological Sourcebook, *Violence against Women and Children*, edited by Carol J. Adams and Marie M. Fortune, an essay written by Emilie Townes, entitled, "Washed in the Grace of God," discusses the importance of speaking out against domestic violence. Emile Townes posits that:

> Black folk need to work with Black folk to help create positive images of male and female that are not dominated by someone else's version of who we are. We must become each other's harvest and in doing so, we will begin to recognize the gift of life we have in each other and turn away from battering ourselves into victim age. One place to begin to gain these new images is in the life of a church that no longer condones business as usual or transmits

---

[20] Meg Kennedy Dugan and Roger R. Hock, *It's My Life Now: Starting over After an Abusive Relationship or Domestic Violence* (New York, NY: Routledge, 2006) xi.

[21] Sharon Ellis Davis, *Battered African American Women: A Study of Gender Entrapment* (Lewiston, NY: Edwin Mellen Press, 2014), 99.

religiousized versions of domination and subordination.[22]

How many churches have you attended that advocate against domestic violence? How many preachers have you heard preach a sermon on domestic violence? When has the church took a stand against the prevalent issue of domestic violence? The church must take the lead in shattering the silence on domestic violence. We must advocate against these injustices and hold each other accountable for our actions. Townes further posits that:

> We must engage in community-building work that ministers to our souls, lifts our spirits (individually and collectively), assures our connection with each other and to God, and pulls us beyond ourselves. The Black religious community needs to create large spaces of welcome, understanding, and confrontation from the pulpit to its religious programming. Folks need to hear the church say in a clear and unequivocal voice that sexual and domestic violence are not acceptable behaviors but they are lethal values.[23]

There resources will help to fill the void created by a lack of support measures for domestic violence victims in churches; a void that has been shaped as a result of the church's silence and neglect to act on the issue. Steven R. Tracy, in "Clergy Responses to Domestic Violence," writes "while some clergy say very incorrect and harmful things in response to abuse, they are often silent about what does need to be said, namely, that God hates abuse and that domestic violence is sinful and unacceptable. This message is not only urgent for entire congregations, but it can be particularly empowering for abuse victims."[24] It is time for churches to stand their ground, alleviate the air of secrecy and address the prevalent issues of guilt and shame that many survivors of domestic violence are experiencing.

Guilt impacts domestic violence victims and survivors on a daily basis and permeates all that we do. Many survivors of domestic violence remain in abusive relationships too long as a result of feeling guilty and trapped. I remained in my abusive relationship too long for the same reasons. Guilt is when one believes, accurately or inaccurately, that one's standards has been compromised or violated and bears the responsibility of the violation. In essence, guilt for me was bearing

[22] Emile Townes, "Washed in the Grace of God," in *Violence Against Women and Children*, ed. Carol Adams and Marie Fortune (New York: Continuum, 1998), 69.

[23] Ibid., 69.

[24] Steven R. Tracey, "Clergy Responses to Domestic Violence," *Mending the Soul* (blog). April 2007 (accessed May 18, 2013), http://www.mendingthesoul.org/2007/04/clergy-responses-to-domestic-violence/.

the responsibility of doing or not doing something right which triggered my abuse. There were many times when I questioned myself thinking, "If I had only done or not done this or that, this wouldn't be happening to me." After every abusive episode, I felt guilty. I wanted so bad to change me, change him, and change the situation. And I could not. I felt helpless.

Ty C. Colbert, a licensed clinical psychologist, classifies guilt into two types of emotions: true and false guilt. "The key to distinguishing true from false guilt is whether the action was intentional. In other words, you are not guilty of any wrongdoing unless you intentionally chose to do something wrong."[25] Colbert posits that a real acquainted sense of false guilt is derived "when others attempt to control us or belittle us by making us feel inadequate, guilty or bad about ourselves."[26] One can see from Colbert's explanation that the guilt experienced by survivors of domestic violence falls into the category of false guilt. Abuse is never justified and there is nothing you and I can do to cause the violence. The batterer has chosen to abuse based on misuse of power and control. I did not have Ty C. Colbert book in my possession as I was going through abuse. While I was a victim of domestic violence, I did not want any action of mines to trigger the abuse and because I did not know what the triggers were, they differ from time to time; I lead a cautious life, which affected every aspect of my actions from reading, watching television, cooking, listen to music, etc. I was a prisoner in my own home.

Andrew Sung Park explained my feeling in his work, *From Hurt to Healing: A Theology of the Wounded*. In this work, Park introduces a Korean term, *han*, and writes, "*han* is the rupture of the soul caused by abuse, exploitation, injustice and violence. When the soul is hurt so much, it bursts symbolically; it aches. When the aching soul is wounded again by external violence, the victim suffers yet a deeper ache. The wound produced by such repeated abuse and injustice is *han* in the depth of the soul."[27] Repetitive abuse, thus, ruptures the soul internally. Park further distinguishes the difference between guilt experienced by wrongdoers versus those who have been wronged.

> While wrongdoers' guilt is natural, that of the wrong is unnatural. When we commit a sin or wrong another, the guilt we experience over the act is healthy. Unhealthy guilt, on the other hand, arises from a defense mechanism. One of

---

[25] Ty C. Colbert, *Why Do I Feel Guilty When I've Done Nothing Wrong?* (Nashville, TN: Thomas Nelson Publishers, 1993), 9.

[26] Ibid., 15.

[27] Andrew Sung Park, *From Hurt to Healing: A Theology of the Wounded* (Nashville, TN: Abingdon Press, 2004), 11-12.

the symptoms of the wronged is self-blame, shame, and guilt.[28]

Long after my external wounds (scratches, bruises, black eye, etc.) had healed, I still had internal wounds that could not be physically seen with the naked eyes but were manifested on the inside. The scholarship in this chapter supports my case that there are aftereffects of surviving domestic violence and those aftereffects, I posit, cannot be healed in silence but must be healed in a caring community.

Linda Hollis in, *Inner Healing for Broken Vessels*, spoke plainly of my dilemma and the internal wounds of domestic violence survivors by sharing an experience of admiring a beautiful gold vase in a curio shop that was awe inspiring externally, while possessing lines and scratches internally, depicting the designer struggle in fashioning the vase. "Inside was a complexity of lines and scratches. They told a different story than the exterior beauty. They told of the difficulty the designed had while trying to complete the vase."[29] Hollis metaphorically relates the vase to people who look good on the outside but are wounded on the inside. "That vase tells the story of so many of us, who look good and together on the outside but, have wounded interiors. There are designer dresses, shoes, accessories, and perfumes to cover the broken hearts and crushed spirits of women."[30] Survivors of domestic violence and sexual abuse fit this metaphor. Many actresses, movie stars, athletes, business women, parishioners fit this metaphor. I fit this metaphor. As a victim and survivor of domestic violence, there were many instances where I looked woundless externally but was screaming and experiencing pain internally. Having always a love for shopping, I purchased things that made me look good externally (the suits, dresses, shoes, perfume, etc.) while I was wounded deeply on the inside. All of the material possessions gave me temporary satisfaction when what I needed for healing and wholeness. Internal scars, wounds, and hurts are real to domestic violence survivors and my internal scars and wounds were real to me. It was through voice and dialog that these scars, wounds, and hurts were unveiled and I began a process of healing. Healing began, for me, with sharing. I realized what research has always stated: that there is no healing in isolation.

For so long, I felt alone. I distanced myself from others because I felt as though what I was experiencing would come out. I became withdrawn and rigid in my personality. I isolated myself from those who truly loved me. Not only did I have a hard time forgiving others, I had a hard time forgiving myself. I began to internalize the negative verbal abuse received about my body, my capabilities, and

[28] Park, 46.

[29] Linda H. Hollies, *Inner Healing for Broken Vessels: A Domestic Violence Survival Guide* (Cleveland, OH: The Pilgrim Press, 2006) 11-12.

[30] Ibid., 12.

myself. I felt guilty and ashamed. Why should I feel guilty and ashamed when I was not the perpetrator of the violence? Carolyn Akua L. McCrary, Associate Professor of Pastoral Care and Counseling at the Interdenominational Theological Center, writes in her essay, *"Intimate Violence Against Black Women and Internalized Shame: A Womanist Pastoral Counseling Perspective,"* that "shame is an overall self-attribution of failure and 'wrongness.' It is a global self-interpretation that I am wrong I failed. I am bad. Even I am worthless."[31] As a survivor of domestic violence, my philosophy was that I had done something to deserve my abuse and I internalized guilt and shame. Abuse is never justified.

Gershen Kaufman, professor and author of *The Psychology of Shame*, articulates

Shame is a loss of face. ... Shame feels like a wound made from the inside. Shame is dishonor, fallen pride, a broken spirit. The beaten humiliated individual, whether defeated as a child by a brutalizing parent or defeated as an adult by a dead-end career or marriage, has been defeated by shame, has endured it until it has broken the self. If unchecked, shame can engulf the self, immersing the individual deeper into despair. To live with shame is to feel alienated and defeated, never quite good enough to belong. And secretly the self feels to blame; the deficiency lies within. Shame is without parallel a sickness of the soul.[32]

Kaufman gave explanation to my feelings and the feelings of so many other battered women experiencing shame. One must take an introspective look at oneself and make a change. I believe that God will meet us where we are and take us, if we are willing, to another level.

Colbert identifies shame as positive and negative and labels them as either constructive or destructive. According to Colbert, "constructive shame is natural in small amounts and necessary for the proper development of an individual's selfhood and conscience."[33] In essence, Colbert is saying that constructive shame is to our benefit. Colbert states, "constructive shame is beneficial because it helps in our emotional and cognitive growth. Because constructive shame gives us the potential for introspection, it enables us to become more whole."[34] On the other hand,

[31] Carolyn Akua L. McCrary, "Intimate Violence Against Black Women and Internalized Shame: A Womanist Pastoral Counseling Perspective," *The Journal of the ITC 28* (2001): 3-37.

[32] Gershen Kaufman PhD, *The Psychology of Shame: Theory and Treatment of Shame Based Syndromes* (New York, NY: Springer Publishing Company, 1989), 24.

[33] Colbert, 4.

[34] Ibid., 21.

destructive shame, according to Colbert, is "the feelings of worthlessness that result when part of the selfhood has been made unlovable or worthless by a violating act."[35] It is this category, destructive shame, which survivors of domestic violence experience. Survivors of domestic violence have survived violation by an intimate partner and must work through healing of this shame. Colbert further states, "destructive shame is not an extension of the natural shame response, but results from living in a violating world. More precisely, it is caused by the pain that results when one human being hurts another."[36] Destructive shame has a detrimental effect because according to Colbert, destructive shame "is an attack on the selfhood, leaving us feeling bad, dirty, or worthless."[37]

Feelings of guilt and shame are evident in the lives of survivors of domestic violence. Many of the women who have come forward this year revealing sexual misconduct behavior and/or sexual harassment articulated how feelings of guilt and shame served as hindrances in telling their stories sooner. Jan Fable, in an article entitled, "Shame," reveals that "the basic nature of chronic, or excessive shame is that the shamed person believes, at some level that she – or – he should not exist, that she is worthless, defective and an empty human being. This shame is debilitating, toxic and highly destructive. Shame is a spiritual crisis at the very core of one's being."[38]

The spiritual crisis of shame is also documented by Ronald Potter-Efron and Patricia Potter-Efron, in *Letting Go of Shame: Understanding How Shame Affects Your Life*. In this book, they state, "a shamed person also suffers a spiritual crisis in which she feels less than human and cut off from others as well as her Higher Power."[39] Survivors of domestic violence feel detached from God. In sharing her story in Al Miles' *Domestic Violence: What Every Pastor Needs to Know*, one survivor writes, "it's been difficult to reach God."[40] Having been abused by two husbands, this survivor felt that God had abandoned her. John Bradshaw, *in Healing the Shame That Binds You*, identifies "toxic shame as spiritual bankruptcy. 'The kingdom of heaven is within,' says the Scripture. Toxic shame looks to the outside for happiness

---

[35] Ibid., 39.

[36] Colbert, 20.

[37] Ibid., 21.

[38] Jan Fable, "Shame." Forhealing.org. December 29, 2013 (accessed December 29, 2013). http://www.forhealing.org/shame.html/.

[39] Potter-Efron and Potter-Efron, 17.

[40] Miles, 85.

and validation, since the inside is flawed and defective."[41] Fortunately, toxic shame is not eternal and change in the way that survivors of domestic violence view themselves can occur. Bradshaw writes, "the good news is you can recover, uncover, and discover your true self and your personal power. But you must be willing to come out of hiding and embrace your toxic shame."[42] Shame, then, cannot be healed in isolation. Walter Fluker stated in a lecture at McCormick Theological Seminary, "the only cure for shame is compassion and community."[43]

The church must work with survivors of domestic violence to validate their worth, hear their stories, believe them, and work toward a more favorable outcome. The process will entail that survivors of domestic violence share their stories as a means for healing, while church leaders offers support, not condemnation or unsupportive advice. The church, which is designed to be so liberating, has actually become oppressive. This can change. This must change! I believe the oppression is a result of the church's failure to adequately and appropriately address the issues and aftereffects of guilt and shame associated with domestic violence. Truth speaking can be liberating.

Bell Hooks and Tyler Perry are two advocates of speaking truth and its liberating results. According to Hooks, "their healing power can be felt in black women's lives if we dare to look at ourselves, our lives, our experiences and then, without shame, courageously name what we see."[44]

Tyler Perry found compassion, community, and cures for his shame. Tyler Perry, actor, director, screenwriter and survivor of sexual abuse, believes truth speaking to be liberating, understand that healing cannot be accomplished in isolation and is probably best encapsulated in his view that healing for him occurred when he told the **truth** publically on a national televised show of Oprah Winfrey with 200 men who had been sexually abused. Perry stated,

> From the moment, I agreed to do the show until the day I actually did it; I had so much anxiety, so many questions. I wasn't sure I should do it until the second it was over. I mean, the very second, I had spoken my truth; it was as if I had removed a five-ton weight from my chest. I felt as if every bit of evil that

---

[41] John Bradshaw, *Healing the Shame That Binds You.* Expanded ed. (Deerfield Beach, FL: HCI, 2005), 42.

[42] Bradshaw, 28.

[43] Walter Earl Fluker, 2014. Black History Lecture, McCormick Theological Seminary Chicago, IL. February 17, 2014.

[44] Bell Hooks, *Sisters of the Yam: Black Women and Self Recovery,* 2nd ed. (Cambridge, MA: South End Press, 2005), 20.

these molesters had sewn into the inseam of my soul had been ripped away. I was so glad I did it. I felt so much lighter and freer. I didn't realize how much power lay in talking about it. I didn't know that part of lifting my own shame was in using my own voice. Out of all the years of self-work and discovery, I think that moment was the one that did the most good on my journey to healing.[45]

Although Tyler Perry and the other 200 men who spoke publically on the nationally televised Oprah Winfrey show are male survivors, shame knows no gender bounds, ethnicity, race, creed, or color. Shame is experienced by both male and female survivors of domestic violence. Howard Fradkin, a licensed psychologist, advocates "the most likely result of shame is keeping silent about what was done to you."[46] Fradkin further believes that "a group experience would be the most powerful way to help men break their silence, heal their shame and join forces to build a lasting brotherhood capable of providing a lifeline of necessary support."[47] I posit that the same group experience would be powerful for women as well. Fradkin writes "disclosing the secret of your abuse will help you let go of the shame once you feel safe enough to tell your story."[48]

In the latter part of 2017, many, many women came forth sharing the secrets of sexual misconduct by various men, some celebrities, Congressmen, physicians, athletes, and the like. As a means of healing, it is important and imperative that survivors be encouraged to share their stories and dialog about the detrimental feelings and emotions of guilt and shame. Similarly, sharing my own personal story was therapeutic. It allowed me to receive empathy and support from caring peers and to realize that I was not alone. We must show love and acceptance to those who have experienced abuse and be willing to accompany them on their healing journey as they work through the aftereffects of their guilt and shame. Justes in her book, *Please Don't Tell* surmises "we are a bridge for others to be able to receive and accept God's grace and love when we carry a clear awareness of the boundless love of God for ourselves and for others."[49] We must continue the Me Too Movement originated by Tarana Burke supporting the survivors of sexual abuse, assault, harassment, and yes, domestic violence.

---

[45] Howard Fradkin, *Joining Forces: Empowering Male Survivors to Thrive* (Carlsbad, CA: Hay House, 2012), xvi.

[46] Ibid., xx.

[47] Ibid., xxiii.

[48] Ibid., 7-8.

[49] Justes, 128.

What consumes us controls us. The more guilt and shame consumes us, the more guilt and shame controls us; it controls our thinking, our actions, and our emotions. Anything that one will not share keeps one in bondage. I cannot count the number of times that I blamed myself for my situation. My guilt and shame bore a factor on a distorted self-image and was a hindrance, for so long, in my forgiving myself. I was in denial about the guilt and shame that I was experiencing as a result of surviving domestic violence. I had to work through a process of rejecting the blame and transferring it to the appropriate place. I had to acknowledge that the abuse was not my fault. I had to affirm and re-affirm reasons why I should not feel guilty. I had to access what I needed in order to move forward. It was through voice, not hiding what had happened to me, and opening up in peer group sessions that allowed my healing to come to fruition. I found out that I was not alone. I, too, am able to hashtag on social media #MeToo!

The importance of the storytelling theme is also found in *African American Pastoral Care*, where Edward Wimberly outlies the narrative approach to pastoral care. Wimberly states that "stories function in the caring setting to bring healing and wholeness to the lives of persons and families within the black pastoral care context."[50] Wimberly outlies the basis of storytelling and emphasize the necessity also of story-listening. Story-listening, according to Wimberly, involves empathically hearing the story of the person involved in life struggles. Empathy means that we attend to the person with our presence, body posture, and nonverbal responses. It also means using verbal responses to communicate that we have understood and are seeking to understand the person's story as it is unfolding.[51]

Many people are hearing the stories of so many men, women, and girls who have been abused; some for the first time and some have heard their stories before but failed to believe them. We must hear the stories of those courageous and brave enough to tell their stories. Everyone is not courageous and brave enough to share their stories. There are people who died with secrets of domestic violence and sexual abuse occurring to them. Many times years have lapsed, until survivors finally share their stories. So when people are ready to share, let us listen attentively and with a nonjudgmental attitude.

Healing is a process. One must have a strong personal commitment to healing. As survivors of domestic violence it is important to us to receive verbal or cognitive affirmation. Sometimes we need to be reminded of our potential, good qualities and worth as a person. During the healing process there must be cognitive restructuring: positive self-talk and positive thinking. I am loveable. I am confident. I am strong. I am beautiful. We must understand, in healing the emotional pain that

---

[50] Edward P. Wimberly, African American Pastoral Care, rev. ed. (Nashville, TN: Abingdon Press, 2008), 3.

[51] Ibid., 7.

it is alright to cry. We possess, in this healing process, a freedom to be angry but not allow our anger to cause us to sin. It is perfectly okay to be angry about what we experienced. Most of all, I believe, we must have faith in God knowing that God loves us and we were created in the image of God.

As I was walking in a public park one day, God gave me a revelation of healing on broken pieces. I saw a cracked vase with broken pieces all over it. The broken pieces were glued together so that the vase itself was completely whole. People take broken pieces and make vases and other objects. We, in turn, purchase these vases and objects and display them in our homes and offices. The seller gets the profit from the sale and we get the merchandise. It became so clear that if I give God the broken pieces of my life (anger, bitterness, denial, grief, depression, low self-esteem, relationships, finances, marriage, guilt, shame, etc.) and allow God to shape the broken pieces, I would get the benefit of the shaping and God would get the glory. The pace of my walk increased as I received this revelation. I left the park traveling to Hobby Lobby to purchase a vase. I found a brown, broken vase with enough broken pieces to label and displayed it as a visual reminder. I found joy in knowing that I was not an egg or Humpty Dumpty and even though I was broken, God could make me whole.

The next chapter will outline the foundation for addressing this challenging problem through the lens of scripture.

3 THE UNDERGIRDING

This literary work has provided the focus of ministry and clearly points out two of the many aftereffects of surviving domestic violence: guilt and shame. It also implies that rarely are there ministries within the local church to address these aftereffects. The intention of this chapter is to explore from scripture an aged problem and a purposed solution. The Old Testament pericope will clearly portray what happens when the church, pastors, and ministry leaders are silent on the issue of domestic violence and how it affects the one who suffered abuse. Many churches are silent and fail to provide support ministries for survivors of domestic violence. It appears that the church would rather focus on the spiritual while neglecting the physical and thus neglecting to be relevant and address holistic issues. The New Testament pericope will provide a paradigm shift and show that Jesus was concerned about the whole person and performed holistic ministry during his time on earth. Jesus further stated that "we" would do greater works than He did.

Violence against women is not unusual and dates back to biblical times. Renita J. Weems, in *Battered Love*, posits that,

> Violence against women in the Bible is virtually always cast in sexual terms. Women were punished with rape, beatings, exposure of their private parts, and mutilation of their bodies – and often these things take place at the hands of men who are related to them (e.g. Jephthah's daughters in Judges 11; the virgin daughters in Gibeah and the Levite's concubine in Judges 19; or Tamar in 2 Samuel 13). The correlation drawn repeatedly in prophetic literature between divine judgment and husbands battering their wives is haunting and telling. It suggests that as far back as the days of the biblical writings, women in love were women in trouble. At the very best, it should convince those who dismiss feminist criticism of biblical language and biblical patriarchy as lacking depth, inconsequential, and trendy that there is probably more than a chance connection between patriarchy and violence against women.[52]

The Old Testament Scripture is 2nd Samuel 12:1-22 and it states,

Sometime later, this happened: Absalom, David's son, had a sister who was

---

[52] Renita J. Weems, Battered Love: Marriage, Sex, and Violence in the Hebrew Prophets (Minneapolis, MN: Fortress Press, 1995), 2.

very attractive. Her name was Tamar. Amnon, also David's son was in love with her. Amnon was obsessed with his sister Tamar to the point of making himself sick over her. She was a virgin, so he couldn't see how he could get his hands on her. Amnon had a good friend, Jonadab, the son of David's brother Shimeah. Jonadab was exceptionally streetwise. He said to Amnon, "Why are you moping around like this, day after day – you, the son of the king! Tell me what's eating at you." "In a word, Tamar," said Amnon. "My brother Absalom's sister. I'm in love with her." "Here's what to do," said Jonadab. "Go to bed and pretend you're sick. When your father comes to visit you, say, 'have my sister Tamar come and prepare some supper for me here where I can watch her and she can feed me." So Amnon took to his bed and acted sick. When the king came to visit, Amnon said, "Would you do me a favor? Have my sister Tamar come and make some nourishing dumplings here where I can watch her and be fed by her." David sent word to Tamar who was home at the time: "Go to the house of your brother Amnon and prepare a meal for him." So, Tamar went to her brother Amnon's house. She took dough, kneaded it, formed it into dumplings, and cooked them while he watched from his bed. But when she took the cooking pot and served him, he wouldn't eat. Amnon said, "Clear everyone out of the house," and they all cleared out. Then he said to Tamar, "Bring the food into my bedroom, where we can eat in privacy." She took the nourishing dumplings she had prepared and brought them to her brother Amnon in his bedroom. But when she got ready to feed him, he grabbed her and said, "Come to bed with me, sister!" "No, brother!" she said, "Don't hurt me! This kind of thing isn't done in Israel! Don't do this terrible thing! Where would I ever show my face? And you – you'll be out on the street in disgrace. Oh, please! Speak to the king – he'll let you marry me." But he wouldn't listen. Being much stronger than she, he raped her. No sooner had Amnon raped her than he hated her – an immense hatred. The hatred that he felt for her was greater than the love he'd had for her. "Get up," he said, "and get out!" "Oh no, brother," she said. "Please! This is an even worse evil than what you just did to me!" But he wouldn't listen to her. He called for his valet. "Get rid of this woman. Get her out of my sight! And lock the door after her." The valet threw her out and locked the door behind her. She was wearing a long-sleeved gown. (That's how virgin princesses used to dress from early adolescence on.) Tamar poured ashes on her head, then she ripped the long-sleeved gown, held her head in her hands, and walked away, sobbing as she went. Her brother Absalom said to her, "Has your brother Amnon had his way with you? Now, my dear sister, let's keep it quiet – a family matter. He is, after all, your brother. Don't take this so hard." Tamar lived in her brother Absalom's home, bitter and desolate. King David heard the whole story and was enraged, but he didn't discipline Amnon, David doted on him because he was his firstborn.

Absalom quit speaking to Amnon – not a word, whether good or bad – because he hated him for violating his sister Tamar.[53]

Second Samuel 13:1-22 is not a pericope that you will hear preached often in many churches today. It records the narrative, on one occasion, about the reality of domestic violence in the Old Testament. The biblical narrative conveys the aftereffects of domestic violence on the family.

2nd Samuel background

The background to 2nd Samuel is intriguing and is described by John McArthur as follows:

First and Second Samuel were considered as one book in the earliest Hebrew manuscripts. They were later divided into the two books by the translators of the Greek version, the Septuagint (LXX), a division also followed by the Latin Vulgate, English translations, and modern Hebrew Bibles. The earliest Hebrew manuscripts entitled the one book Samuel after the man God used to establish the kingship in Israel. Later Hebrew texts and the English versions call the ancient books 1 and 2 Samuel.[54]

As MacArthur notes, the books span about 135 years of history. During those years, Israel was transformed from a loosely knit group of tribes under judges to a unite nation under the reign of a centralized monarchy. They look primarily at Samuel, Saul who reigned and David who was king of the united monarchy.[55]

MacArthur shares that one of the theological themes of the Books of Samuel is that "the Books of Samuel demonstrate the personal and national effects of sin."[56] In Second Samuel 13:1-22, we see, on one occasion, the reality of domestic violence in the Old Testament. The biblical narrative conveys the aftereffects of domestic violence on the family. David's two sons, Amnon and Absalom, along with his daughter, Tamar, are the focal point of this story. Phyllis Trible describes Amnon as "a prince with power,

---

[53] 2 Samuel 13:1-33 (NRSV)

[54] John MacArthur, The MacArthur Bible Commentary: Unleashing God's Truth One Verse at a Time (Nashville, TN: Thomas Nelson, 2005), 299.

[55] Ibid., 300.

[56] Ibid., 301.

prestige and unrestrained lust,"[57] while describing Tamar as "a princess to whom belong wisdom, courage, and unrelieved suffering."[58]

Detailed Analysis

A summary of the pericope will point out that a familiar, family member, her half-brother, Amnon raped Tamar. Amnon had a lustful appetite for Tamar and desired to lay with her. Their cousin, Jonadab devised a scheme that would put Tamar in Amnon's bedroom at the request of their father, King David. While Tamar was fulfilling a request to cook cakes for her brother Amnon (who had pretended to be ill), he proposed that they have sex. How often in today's society does women, who are trying to be helpful and resourceful, end up being abused and sexually assaulted? How often at the request of family members are young girls put in the hands of perpetrators? Although Tamar resisted the proposition, Amnon forced himself upon her and raped her.

Tamar soon realized that domestic violence aftereffects brought shame. Used and abused, Tamar was driven with her shame from the door of her callous brother. The shame that Tamar experienced could not be hidden, erased, or washed away with soap and water; and feeling humiliated, bruised, bleeding, frustrated, feeling guilty, and shamed as a result, Tamar went into public mourning. Tamar put ashes on her head, tore her long sleeved garment, which symbolized that she was no longer a virgin, place her hands on her head and cried aloud as she ran to her blood brother Absalom's house. Tamar was now a devalued princess, but she did not try to hide what had happened to her; and yet, no one cared. Absalom immediately discerned what had taken place and while Tamar confirmed the abuse, Absalom's insisted that Tamar keep silent. Knowing that his sister had been abused, Absalom only advice to her was to keep silent. Emma Justes in her book, *Please Don't Tell* writes, "the desire to maintain power, image, name and respect drives the need to keep secrets hidden."[59] Absalom's only concern was for secrecy and as a result, Absalom silenced Tamar's voice.

Tamar remained a "desolate" woman in Absalom's house, constantly weeping, and rehearsing the scenes of the rape in her mind. She was

---

[57] Phyllis Trible, Texts of Terror: Literary-Feminist Readings of Biblical Narrative (Philadelphia, PA: Fortress Press, 1984), 37.

[58] Ibid., 37.

[59] Justes, 128.

lifeless, moping about like an empty shell, voiceless, ostracized, guilt ridden and shamed. Justes posits that "for Tamar there would be no voice, no marriage, no children, no respect, and no place except for her space in her brother's house as a desolate woman. We cannot count how many women since Tamar have become desolate women!"[60] And exactly how does this desolation take place? Why, failing to address the issues of guilt and shame for survivors of domestic violence will leave one desolate.

By failing to address the issues of guilt and shame for survivors of domestic violence, the victims will often become desolate as they are forced to live with the shame filled secrets of their abuse. Shame filled secrets that can and should be shared in a church community, to provide the survivor of domestic violence hope and initiate healing. Justes writes that, "the experience of being part of a community can offer an antidote for shame, so one could expect that the church would be the ideal place for the elimination or prevention of secrets."[61]

David found out what happened yet he failed to chastise his son. Interesting to note, both Absalom and David exhibited silence to domestic violence. As King, it was David's responsibility to uphold the law. Leviticus 20:17 state, "if a man marries his sister, whether his father's daughter or his mother's daughter, and they have sexual relations, it is a disgrace. They must be cut off publicly form their people. He has had sexual intercourse with his sister, he will bear his punishment."[62] David failed to uphold this law. As a Father, it was David's responsibility to discipline his son. But David had sinned previously by lusting after and committing adultery with Bathsheba, impregnating her and eventually having her husband Uriah, killed. Justes helps us to understand that "secrecy and violence span generations: David takes Bathsheba and Amnon lays Tamar. Amnon replicates his father's behavior. Where secrets are hidden, similar dynamics often emerge."[63] Amnon was following in David's footsteps. If David had upheld the law, Amnon would have been banned from Israel and held accountable for his actions. David was the father of Tamar and Amnon, the abused and the abuser. MacArthur notes that "fury and indignation were David's reaction to the report of rape. Because he did not punish Amnon for his crime, he abdicated his responsibility both as king and as father. The lack of justice in the land would come back to haunt David in a

---

[60] Justes, 131.

[61] Ibid., 134.

[62] Leviticus 20:17 (Holman Christian Standard Bible)

[63] Justes, 131.

future day."[64] The biblical narrative does not record where David showered Tamar with love and compassion but reveals David's anger and silence. David did nothing to console his daughter or discipline his son.

Phyllis Trible states, "David's anger signifies complete sympathy for Amnon and total disregard for Tamar. How appropriate that the story never refers to David and Tamar as father and daughter! The father identifies with the son; the adulterer supports the rapist; male has joined male to deny justice for the female."[65] Most fathers have or desire a positive, loving relationship with their daughters. A father's relationship in his daughter's life shapes her opinion of men, self-image and self-esteem.

The aftereffects of domestic violence are far reaching and affect the survivor but also children, families, churches, and society as a whole. Tamar remained barren, unloved, and unable to marry or be given in marriage. She had been violated, abused, and nothing is ever mentioned of her again in Scripture. There is an internalization of shame. Kaufman states that, "it is through imagery (encompassing visual, auditory, and kinesthetic dimensions) that the self internalizes experience. What are internalized are images or scenes that have become imprinted with affect."[66] Tamar exhibited low self-esteem and like other survivors of domestic violence, rehearsed negative scenes over and over again in her mind. Scott Tatum in, *The Teacher's Commentary* states, "the circumstances of domestic violence may vary; nonetheless, the results are always the same – guilt, shame, hatred and death."[67] I disagree with hatred and death always being results of domestic violence; however, I do believe that all survivors of domestic violence experience some degree of guilt and shame.

Tamar lived the remainder of her life not realizing that she was fearfully and wonderfully made. Tamar was now disqualified from marriage because she was no longer a virgin, an identity taken from her by force. Tamar was not made aware that her father loved her or that God loved her.

Tamar's story must never be diminished, dismissed or forgotten. Tamar's story is the rape of Dinah in Genesis 34 story. Pamela Cooper White in her book, *The Cry of Tamar*, shares how the story of Tamar is still

---

[64] MacArthur, 370.

[65] Trible, 53-54.

[66] Kaufman, 58-59.

[67] Scott L. Tatum, "2 Samuel" in, *The Teacher's Bible Commentary*, ed. Franklin H. Paschall and Herchel H. Hobbs (Nashville, TN: Broadman and Holman Publishers, 1972), 187.

relevant today when she writes,

- Tamar was sexually assaulted, not by a stranger, but by someone she knew.
- The violation took place not in the dark alley or in a desolate park, but by a member of her own family, at home.
- Tamar was exploited through one of her most vulnerable traits – her kindness and her upbringing to take care of others.
- Tamar said "no," her "no" was not respected.
- When Tamar sought help, she was told to keep quiet.
- The process for achieving justice and restitution was taken out of her hands entirely and carried forward by her brother – it became men's business.
- In the end, it was her perpetrator for whom her father mourned, not for her.
- The end of Tamar's story happens without her.[68]

Tamar's story is my story. And unfortunately, Tamar's story is the story of many, many other abused, voiceless women. *Where was the church in Tamar's abuse? Where was the King? Where was God? Who was speaking out? Who is speaking up against the crime and injustice of domestic violence?*

Tamar's story vividly shows what happens when we fail to address our aftereffects of guilt, shame, anger, denial, grief, and low self-esteem. The outcome of Tamar's life should have been different. The outcome of Tamar's life could have been different. The outcome of your life can be different.

New Testament Foundation
A New Paradigm

In the New Testament, Luke 4:18-19 provides a model to churches for alleviating silence and opening up space to address the aftereffects of guilt and shame for survivors of domestic violence.

The Spirit of the Lord is on me, because he has anointed me to proclaim good news to the poor. He has sent me to proclaim favor for the prisoners and recovery of sight for the blind, to set the oppressed

---

[68] Pamela Cooper-White, *The Cry of Tamar: Violence Against Women and the Church's Response*, 2 ed. (Minneapolis, MN: Fortress Press, 2012), 29.

free, to proclaim the year of the Lord's favor.[69]

Luke Background

According to Youngblood, "Luke was written by a Gentile for Gentiles."[70] Luke, as the author, does not identify himself by name; nonetheless, identification came from early church fathers. "Writing about A.D. 175, Irenaeus, bishop of Lyon, identified the author as Luke, the companion of Paul. Eusebius agreed adding that Luke was a native of Antioch."[71]

MacArthur shares that "a running theme in Luke's Gospel is Jesus' compassion for Gentiles, Samaritans, women, children, tax collectors, sinners, and others often regarded as outcasts in Israel."[72] Women, the largest percentage of survivors of domestic violence is considered outcasts. Yet, Luke shows and "emphasizes the central role of women in the life and ministry of our Lord."[73] Jesus does care about women. Jesus cares about you and Jesus cares about me.

Detailed Analysis

A summary of the pericope will show that Jesus was in attendance at synagogue worship. A synagogue in Jesus' time can be compared to our local church. Jesus was invited to read the scripture. Knowles states that, "He chooses part of Isaiah, where the prophet is announcing that God will rescue his people. He describes something like a Jubilee, when invalids are healed, debts cancelled and prisoners released (Isaiah 61:1–9). Sitting down to teach, Jesus says simply, 'this is happening now—before your very eyes. I am the Jubilee!'"[74] My own case has driven urgency for this work, for I understand that even after ending the abusive relationship, residual guilt and

---

[69] Luke 4:18-19 (NIV).

[70] Ronald F. Youngblood, *Nelson's New Illustrated Bible Dictionary* (Nashville, TN: Nelson Publishers, 1995), 778.

[71] Ibid., 778.

[72] MacArthur, 1265.

[73] Ibid., 1266.

[74] Andrew Knowles, *The Bible Guide*, 1st Augsburg books ed. (Minneapolis, MN: Augsburg Books, 2001), 476.

shame still have to be addressed. Left unaddressed, guilt and shame will have a detrimental effect on the survivor of domestic violence and continued victimization is likely to occur.

There are six themes in this pericope: The Spirit of the Lord is on me (first theme); because he has anointed me to proclaim good news to the poor (second theme). He has sent me to proclaim favor for the prisoners (third theme) and recovery of sight for the blind (fourth theme), to set the oppressed free (fifth theme), to proclaim the year of the Lord's favor (sixth theme).

The first theme states that God with the Holy Spirit has anointed Jesus for service. Nolland states, "the Spirit is upon Jesus by reason of the anointing that occurred at his baptism."[75] Anointing provides power and presence of God to do the task that God has set before you. Spragin contends that:

> The indication is that this anointing is to a place of both prominence and permanence. Thus, Jesus was saying that he had already been chosen and anointed by God for not just the tasks, but also more specifically, the office which he now held, which held the responsibility of the tasks he would perform. This event in the synagogue was the public announcement of that anointing.[76]

As pastors, laity, and ministry leaders who are anointed by God, we have the power and presence of the Holy Spirit to provide ministries within our church that addresses the aftereffects of guilt and shame as a result of surviving domestic violence. We should not shrink from our responsibility. Jesus never did!

Clark explains the second theme of being anointed to bring good news to the poor:

> The recipients of the good news were the poor and oppressed. Part of following Jesus meant accepting the ministry that he practiced. Evangelism meant bringing the good news to the poor, outcast and oppressed. If this is evangelism, then isn't addressing spousal and child abuse also part of evangelism? Shouldn't the church be concerned

---

[75] John Nolland, *Word Biblical Commentary Vol 35a, Luke 1:1-9:20* (Dallas, TX: Thomas Nelson, 1989), 196.

[76] Ore Lee Spragin, Jr., *Commentary on the Gospel of Luke* (n/p: CreateSpaceIndependent Publishing Platform, 2011), 57.

about domestic violence? Even more, if twenty-five percent of women in America have been physically abused, how many people could we reach if we began to address domestic violence?[77]

In essence, Clark is stating that when the church fails to address domestic violence, it fails to perform evangelism. "All people need Jesus, Jesus came to preach good news to the poor and oppressed. Evangelism means that we practice Jesus' ministry by bringing freedom and justice to all people who are oppressed, whether we consider them in or out of the church."[78]

Theme three of proclaiming favor to prisoners can be best described as being rescued from oppressive situations. Nolland states, "it is widely agreed that the language of Jubilee release is being picked up in Isaiah 61:1-2."[79] The year of Jubilee was a time period where prisoners were freed, debt cancelled, and complete rest for the land. Survivors of domestic violence are in bondage to the aftereffects of guilt and shame and in need of being released. Jesus proclaimed that he came for that reason – to release prisoners from whatever captivity they found themselves, not just in the year of Jubilee but always, continuously.

The recovery of sight to the blind in theme four can be seen as healing, both physically and spiritually. To many of the physically blind, Jesus gave the gift of sight; however, on one occasion in the healing of the blind man in Luke 18:35-42, Jesus pronounced healing and salvation when he proclaimed, "Go ahead—see again! Your faith has saved and healed you!"[80]

Discussion of theme five will show that this pericope is focusing of relieving people of pain associated with being in captivity. The people had been waiting for a Messiah to deliver them from Roman oppression. Jesus proclaimed, in this pericope, that the people need look no further. Their Messiah had come. And as a result of his coming, the captives would be set free. Clark states, "If the church is going to be like Jesus, it must be prophetic."[81] This means that the church's praxis must be social justice. "The Jesus in Luke's gospel was prophetic in that he called the early

---

[77] Clark, 234.

[78] Ibid., 235.

[79] Nolland, 197.

[80] Luke 18:42 (The Message Bible)

[81] Clark, 236.

Christians to practice social justice."[82] Jesus is still calling his church of today to practice social justice, as "Jesus the prophet challenged those in power to attend to the needs of victims."[83] We must practice or demonstrate what we have learned.

In theme six, Jesus announced that the year of Jubilee had arrived. "Domestic violence victims and their children suffer tremendous scars and shame from their trauma and experiences. The church has the opportunity to enter their lives and aggressively love them and remind them that they have hope in God."[84] God has called the church to take the lead in assisting survivors of domestic violence with the aftereffects of guilt and shame.

The model for this project depends on this particular passage because it shows that the church can no longer stand on the side line when addressing the relevant issues of those who worship within, to include addressing the aftereffects of guilt and shame associated with survivor domestic violence. The year of the Lord's favor for survivors of domestic violence is NOW! Now is the acceptable time for the church to establish ministries for survivors of domestic violence. Or better yet, in the African sense of urgency, it's NOW NOW time! There is urgency in ministries within the local church to address domestic violence.
Craddock substantiates the urgency of now being the proper time when he states:

> It is interesting that in Luke's Gospel, the first public work of Jesus as an adult apart from reading Scripture is today. The age of God's reign is here; the eschatological time when God's promises are fulfilled and God's purpose comes to fruition has arrived; those changes for the poor and the wronged and the oppressed will come today. This is the beginning of Jubilee. The time of God is today, and the ministries of Jesus and the Church according to Luke-Acts demonstrates today continued.[85]

In essence, Craddock is saying that God still expects the church to be the church of social justice today. This means that pastors, ministry leaders,

---

[82] Ibid., 237.

[83] Clark, 238.

[84] Ibid., 250.

[85] Fred B. Craddock, *Interpretation Luke: A Bible Commentary for Teaching and Preaching* (Louisville, KY: John Knox Press, 1990), 62.

and churches must publically take a stand against abuse and domestic violence today and work towards healing of guilt and shame for survivors of domestic violence.

Theological Foundations

Who is God to survivors of domestic violence? James Cone in his book, *God of the Oppressed*, writes "to affirm that liberation is an expression of the image of God is to say not only who God is but also who I am and who my people are. Liberation is knowledge of self; it is a vocation to affirm who I am created to be."[86] Thus, liberation is transformation. Survivors of domestic violence must alter their thinking and behavior to alleviate feelings of guilt and shame. They must know God as a God who is on their side for healing and releasing of oppression.

Furthermore, since I believe that liberation theology's goal is equality – equality that refutes the various ism's (racism, sexism, classism, genderism, etc.), I invite Elizabeth Cady Stanton into this dialogue as she reflects, from a feminist perspective, on God. Stanton, in *The Woman's Bible*, articulates "God create man in his own image, male and female. Thus Scripture, as well as science and philosophy, declares the eternity and equality of sex."[87] Stanton further articulates that Genesis 1:26-27,

> Plainly show the simultaneous creation of man and woman, and their equal importance in the development of the race. All those theories based on the assumption that man was prior in the creation, have no foundation in Scripture. As to woman's subjection, on which both the canon and the civil law delight to dwell, it is important to note that equal dominion is given to woman over every living thing, but not one word is said giving man dominion over woman.[88]

Survivors of domestic violence must negate the male headship/female submission embedded theology that most pastors preach and teach. This theology defines male as head of household and thus privilege to do with females as they please—even to abuse them—while females are obligated to submit to their husbands. Survivors of domestic violence must switch their

---

[86] James H. Cone, *God of the Oppressed*, rev. ed. (Maryknoll, NY: Orbis Books, 1997), 134.

[87] Elizabeth Cady Stanton, *The Woman's Bible: A Classic Feminist Perspective* (Mineola, NY: Dover Publications, 2003), 14-15.

[88] Ibid., 15.

theology to deliberative and disagree with male headship/female submission model. One survivor of domestic violence has testified that she stayed in abusive relationships far too long "believing the abuse was caused by not submitting fully to her husband's authority."[89] It is this kind of thinking that must be changed.

Cone further suggests that "the key to black theology is its refusal to embrace any concept of God which makes black suffering the will of God."[90] The God personified in Cone's work is a God of Liberation. It is never God's will for survivors of domestic violence to remain in bondage to guilt and shame or any bondage at all.

Gustavo Gutiérrez, in *A Theology of Liberation*, specifies that "liberation emphasizes that human beings transform themselves by conquering their liberty throughout their existence and their history."[91] Gutiérrez asserts that God is manifested in Liberation Theology as a God whose self-revelation begins with the mission of liberation. Gutiérrez argues that to know God is to do justice.[92] God is a God of Justice. Gutiérrez says that "the God of Biblical revelation is known through inter-human justice. When justice does not exist, God is not known; God is absent."[93] The church can no longer remain silent on the issue of domestic violence and simultaneously proclaim that they are representing a God of Justice. It refutes the message. If we believe that God is a God of justice then we must put our belief to action.

Jacquelyn Grant in her article, *Womanist Theology in North America* states that "Womanist Theology is a theological perspective that emerges out of the experiences of Black women."[94] Grant further states that "when Black women say that God is on the side of the oppressed, we mean that God is in solidarity with the struggles of those on the underside of humanity."[95]

---

[89] Miles, 31.

[90] James H. Cone, *Black Theology and Black Power* (Maryknoll, NY: Orbis Books, 1997), 124.

[91] Gustavo Gutiérrez, *A Theology of Liberation: History, Politics, and Salvation*, ed. Sister Caridad Inda and John Eagleson (Maryknoll, NY: Orbis Books, 1988), xiv.

[92] Ibid., 110.

[93] Ibid., 111.

[94] Jacquelyn Grant, "Womanist Theology in North America", *Journal of the Interdenominational Theological Center* 16, no. 1-2 (Fall-Spring 1988-1989), 285.

[95] Jacquelyn Grant, *White Women's Christ and Black Women's Jesus: Feminist Christology and Womanist Response* (Atlanta, GA: Scholars Press, 1989), 209.

Many survivors of domestic violence struggle with the emotional bondage of guilt and shame having lived on the underside of humanity. Domestic violence is inhumane. We have an assurance that God is on our side as survivors of domestic violence because domestic violence is a sin. We must teach this womanist theology to survivors of domestic violence as a mean of liberation.

In, *Sisters in the Wilderness*, Deloris Williams describes,

> Womanist theology as a prophetic voice reminding African-American denominational churches of their mission to seek justice and voice for all their people, of which Black women are the overwhelming majority of their congregations. Yet this prophetic voice is concerned about the well-being of the entire African-American community, female and male, adults and children.[96]

Although Williams is speaking about the African-American community, the prophetic voice of all churches must remember its mission of justice and for all survivors of domestic violence. Though this project demographically will be comprised of women survivors of domestic violence who experience guilt and shame; there are also male survivors of domestic violence who also have aftereffects of guilt and shame relevant to domestic violence, who's demographic, is not a component of this research.

Cheryl Kirk-Duggan posits in, *Violence and Theology*, "before we can ever change anything with the preponderance of violence, we must admit that it exists. We must name it and claim our participation before we can transform violence and create a better world." [97] It is imperative to name the aftereffects of guilt and shame of survivors of domestic violence, openly address those issues and stop pretending that they do not exist. We must admit that domestic violence is the elephant in the sanctuary. We must admit that domestic violence exists among our parishioners and be willing to do something about it.

Bell Hooks, in *Sisters of the Yam*, states that "there is no healing in silence."[98] Hooks writes,

---

[96] Delores Williams, *Sisters in the Wilderness* (Maryknoll, NY: Orbis Books, 1999), xii-xiv.

[97] Cheryl A. Kirk-Duggan, *Violence and Theology* (Nashville: Abingdon Press, 2006), 82.

[98] Hooks, 16.

In Alice Walker's novel *The Color Purple*, Celie, the black heroine, only begins to recover from her traumatic experiences of incest/rape, domestic violence, and marital rape when she is able to tell her story, to be open and honest. Reading fictional narratives where black female characters break through silences to speak the truth of their lives, to give testimony, has helped individual black women take the risk to openly share painful experiences. We see examples of such courageous testimony in *The Black Women's Health Book*. Yet many black readers of Alice Walker's fiction were angered by Celie's story. They sought to 'punish' Walker by denouncing the work, suggesting it represented a betrayal of blackness. If this is the way folks respond to fiction, we can imagine then how much harder it is for black women to actually speak honestly in daily life about their real traumatic experiences. And yet there is no healing in silence.[99]

There are many more references that document the belief of healing through storytelling. Of a particular note, Teresa E. Snorton's article, "What About All Those Angry Black Women?" in *Women Out of Order*, highlights theologian Evelyn Parker's challenge to the black church:

> In light of the realities of racism, sexism, and classism, if the church – in which women and girls have long been the majority – is to be a relevant institution, then the church must discern ways to let girls tell their stories and receive God's miraculous healing in the process.[100]

Snorton further articulates that "when working with African-American women, we must be willing to hear their stories, to see their anger, to assist them in naming the anger, and to walk with them through the anger as a means of empowerment and a vehicle for growth."[101]

In conclusion, this project demographically will be composed of African-Americans; however, survivors of domestic violence are composed of all ethnicity and races. Al Miles in *Domestic Violence: What Every Pastor Needs to Know* interviewed "fifty-two survivors of domestic violence who were African-American, Caucasian, Chinese, Filipina, Hispanic, Japanese,

---

[99] Ibid.

[100] Jeanne Stevenson-Moessner, Teresa Snorton, and editors, *Women Out of Order: Risking Change and Creating Care in a Multicultural World* (Minneapolis, MN: Fortress Press, 2010), 217.

[101] Stevenson-Moessner, 217.

Korean, Native Hawaiian, Native American and Samoan."[102]   Domestic violence is an epidemic. "The Federal Bureau of Investigation reports that while 3,200 servicemen were killed in battle between 2000 and 2006, there were 10,600 domestic homicides in the United States, 85 percent of these victims were women."[103]

Similarly, Miles writes, "domestic violence ranks as the number one public health problem for women in America, and yet those of the cloth prefer to look the other way."[104] Domestic violence ranks terribly high as a health problem, yet the institution that is supposed to be so liberating actually ignores the problem. As Martin Luther King, Jr., penned in his twenty-one page letter from the Birmingham Jail, "injustice anywhere is a threat to justice everywhere."[105]   Injustice for survivors of domestic violence in the African-American community is also a threat to survivors in the Caucasian, Chinese, Filipina, Hispanic, Japanese, Korean, Native Hawaiian, Native American and Samoan communities. Failure to address the after effects of guilt and shame in the African-American community is a threat to the failure to address the after effects of guilt and shame in the Caucasian, Chinese, Filipina, Hispanic, Japanese, Korean, Native Hawaiian, Native American and Samoan communities, as well. I decree that justice roll down like a mighty river worldwide.

The methodology used in reframing guilt and shame for women survivors of domestic violence is storytelling. Let the reframing of guilt and shame with survivors of domestic violence begin and let it begin in the church!

---

[102] Miles, 77-78.

[103] Carter, 143.

[104] Miles, 5.

[105] Ali Ali-Dinar, "Letter from the Birmingham Jail [King, Jr.]," African Studies Center University of Pennsylvania, December 30, 2013, accessed December 30, 2013, http://www.africa.upenn.edu/Articles_Gen/Letter_Birmingham.html.

4 THE APPROACH

Hypothesis

One of the most crucial times for survivors of domestic violence occurs after the abusive relationship has ended. Among the many emotions experienced by survivors are guilt and shame, the foci of this project. The hypothesis for this project is that survivors of domestic violence can be supported in the local church and resourced for conquering the emotions of guilt and shame, with a model that advocates storytelling. Sessions were hosted in a specially designated space within the local church that was conducive to sharing the aftereffects of guilt and shame.

The desired results included a reframing of the manner in which survivors of domestic violence thought about themselves and a transferring of the experiences of guilt and shame to the appropriate place. Additionally, the desired outcomes were also for members of the peer focus group to name 'guilt' and 'shame' as two aftereffects of their experienced domestic violence, for them to work through these emotions by sharing their stories thus enabling them to embark upon the journey of healing those emotions, and for them to gain a new positive self-image and boost their self-esteem while peeling off the layers of guilt and shame.

Research Design

This qualitative study employs ethnographic methods of focus groups, observations and surveys. The focus group is intended to be composed of five survivors of domestic violence, for participation in six sessions that are each four hours in duration. There will be a session evaluation with each focus group participant, which will be used in fine-tuning the final design of the model for future use. The findings will aid the implementation of domestic violence support ministries for use by churches.

Measurement

There were two proposed concepts to be measured in this study: guilt and shame of domestic violence survivors. Both concepts were measured utilizing a continuum model comprised of pre-test, observations, and post-test tools to assess the degree of guilt and shame that each participant had at the onset of group versus the degree at the end of the six sessions. The pre-test and post-test continuum tools served as a means for naming the degree of guilt and shame experienced by survivors of domestic violence at two different stages. Levels on the continuum ranged from zero to ten with levels represented as follows: zero being healed; one to four, mild affect; five to seven, moderate affect; and eight to ten, extreme affect. In addition, a pre-survey and post-survey were administered to ascertain the presence of guilt and shame in each participant. Through the pre-survey, I anticipated finding that the women were suffering with guilt and shame as a result of surviving domestic violence, making them viable participants for the study. A model was solidified for use with the peer focus group. This model will be the focus of Chapter Five: Field Experience., The Antidote.

5 THE ANTIDOTE

Five women participated in four hours peer group sessions for six weeks at the local church. Attending the session were participants from both Baptist and Methodist denominations, and only two participants from the host church. Demographic information and confidentiality statements were completed at Session 1. Participants are identified by numbers.

A pre-test and post-test continuum was utilized to measure the degree of guilt and shame of each participant at the onset of peer group sessions and also at the end in Session 6. The range on the continuum ranges on a scale of zero to ten, with zero being healed and ten being extreme feelings of guilt and shame. The following table represents the results of the pre-test continuum. As shown in table below, the table reveals the degree of guilt and shame current in the lives of the survivors of domestic violence participants. Three of the five women survivor participants entered the focus group acknowledging that they were experiencing guilt and shame as a result of surviving domestic violence.

Participant	Guilt	Shame
#7	9	8
#14	0	0
#20	3	3
#55	0	0
#3286	5	6

Session One continued with introductions and a stone exercise used to describe what each participant was currently feeling. Session One ended with each participant articulating their reasons for participating.

Session Two

Each participant was given the opportunity to verbally check in and articulate their current feelings, express feelings about the last session and to share any other pertinent information. The term "guilt" was defined. Journals were distributed to each participant. Writing is another art used in the therapeutic process of sharing. This session focused on role playing, the ways in which we misplace blamed, examine victim blaming language like "it's my fault," or "I provoked it," and means for rejecting and transferring the blame to the appropriate place. Time was allocated for participants to write in their journals with four open ended phrases or sentences. The phrases and sentences were: 1) Never again...; 2) I acknowledge that the abuse was not my fault...;3) I should not feel guilty because....; and 4) In order to move forward, I need....

Session Three

The term shame was defined. Time was allocated for writing in journals focusing on the following questions: Do you feel shamed about what happened to you? Have you ever experienced: Isolation? Felt all alone? Low self-esteem? Hopeless? Unworthy of love? In your experience of feeling shame, did you feel cut off from God? Time was allotted for sharing by each participant. The poem, "We Wear the Mask" by Paul Laurence Dunbar was read. Group participants were directed to place the mask over their faces and focus for the next five minutes on one incident that caused them to feel ashamed. Participants shared their incidents. This exercise was important because emphasis was placed on using the senses, in this case, feeling and hearing, which can be empowering for healing. Ten "I AM" positive affirmations were written and affirmed. This served as a continuous way of internalizing positive affirmations to help negate those previous negative affirmations. Applying the arts in healing are an integral part of this model and thus the focus group participants were encouraged to compose a song, dance or poem that spoke specifically to them expressing their feelings about their new emerging self-image.

Session Four

Storytelling was introduced and reiterated how research had shown that storytelling is vital for healing. All focus group participants shared their stories in their own way, some slowly, some intermingled with tears. Intertwined between stories were music and an opportunity to process. Of all the sessions, Session Four was the most emotional and extended past our allocated time. There were many hugs and positive affirmations provided to focus group participants after they shared.

Session Five

Session Five was on self-esteem utilizing a handout entitled, "Loving the You God Created: Re-evaluating Self-Esteem." A mirror exercise was completed where participants took five minutes to look at themselves in the mirror. After the five minutes had elapsed, we were to draw a picture of ourselves which represented what we saw in the mirror. Participants were invited to share their portrait and elaborate on its meaning. Self-esteem was explained and shared that our self-esteem has been shaped by the messages that we have received and internalized from others. In an effort to pursue new paths, change the distorted views we have of ourselves, and see ourselves as God sees us, eleven self-talk declarations were presented. They are:

- Accept Yourself
- Thank God for Encouraging You
- Accept the Compliments of Others
- Release Past Negative Experiences and Focus on a Positive Future
- Live in God's Forgiveness
- Benefit from Mistakes
- Form Supportive, Positive Relationships
- Formulate Realistic Goals and Plans
- Identify Your Heart's Desires
- Plan for Success
- Celebrate Each Accomplishment[106]

The final exercise in Session Five would begin in Session Five with the intentions of lasting for a minimum of forty days. In this final exercise, participants were asked to look in the mirror and follow a four-step process. The steps are:

1. Say your name
2. Appreciate yourself for
   a. Achievements (business, financial, educational, personal and emotional)
   b. Disciplines kept (exercise, meditation, prayers, eating well)
   c. Say, "I Love you!"
   d. Take it in and receive it: breathe[107]

Gift bags filled with a "Woman of God" mini mirror, an empowering card, a pen with the word "Princess" inscribed and a devotional book entitled, "Beloved Names of God" were distributed to each participant.

Session Six

The post-test continuum survey was completed by participants. The results are outline in Table Two. As shown in Table Two below, the degree of guilt and shame experienced by focus group participants decreased after completing six sessions. The results in the table indicated that the focus group participants benefited from the group

---

[106] Adrian C. Evans, Loving the You God Created: Reevaluating Self-Esteem (Mobile, AL, 2014), 2.

[107] Evans, 4.

session and that there was a realized benefit of decrease in the account of guilt and shame they now felt. In essence, the focus group participants felt better about themselves and realized a boost in self-esteem.

Participant	Guilt	Shame
#7	2	1
#14	Not completed	Not completed
#20	2	2
#55	Not completed	Not completed
#3286	3	3

The focus group was successful in that it was held in a local church setting allowing the women in the focus group to know that as an ambassador of God, I was not afraid to address the relevant issue of guilt and shame associated with surviving domestic violence. Although many churches in the area do not address the issue, having the focus group at the local church showed a willingness to break the silence on domestic violence and provide support to those women who have survived domestic violence. Secondly, the project was successful in that the degree of guilt and shame experienced by focus group participants changed after completing six sessions. The degree on the scale decreased 100% for all respondents, showing that the level of guilt and shame experienced at the onset was quite different at the end. Thirdly, the model of using storytelling as a tool for speaking out about the issues of abuse, experiences encountered, and addressing the issues of guilt and shame was rewarding and successful.

The same positive results of healing initiated after telling one's story is also documented by women in Nancy Werking Poling' book, *Victim to Survivor*. Although the stores were not all shared in focus group settings, the women were able to begin healing after speaking out about their abuse and thus their stories became healing agents for others. The following excerpts from the women demonstrate the results.

Speaking out opened the door to healing, to love and compassion, and to mercy and forgiveness for myself and ultimately for others.[108]

---

[108] Nancy Werking Poling, ed. *Victim to Survivor: Women Recovering from Clergy Sexual Abuse* (N/A: Wipf & Stock Pub., 2009), 21.

I speak out today, because the silence and secrecy of abuse have taken the lives of victims who did not experience the support they wanted and needed in their journey to healing.[109]

There is life after abuse, but I found it by going through it instead of around it. Just as my counselor advised me. I had to face it and live with the ugly implications: being blamed, shamed, taunted and teased. If I can find healing, most people can.[110]

I used to know God through the voice of a "man of God" and through his interpretations of scripture. I now know God in many other ways. I know God through my clients' lives and their stories of suffering and healing…And I know God through the church's willingness to seek justice.[111]

The accounts of these women stories were women recovering from clergy sexual abuse and all have aftereffects of guilt and shame, along with various other residual emotional burdens. Marie Fortune stated,

The miracle of these stories (and the hundreds more like them) is that these women are the church, the broken body of Christ seeking to be made whole through the courage to demand justice. In their pain, these women call upon the church to be the church, and they really expect those of us in the institutional church to rise to the occasion.[112]

In addition to the strengths noted, there were clearly challenges. Two of the five women in the group considered themselves already healed and did not finish the entire six sessions. They dropped out of the group after session three. Their reasoning ranged from work schedule conflicts to attending funerals. However, one of the two dropouts wanted to return for session six for the Mary Kay pampering session.

Secondly, the three women previously identified in the congregation of

[109] Poling, 38.

[110] Ibid., 59.

[111] Ibid., 119-120.

[112] Ibid., ix.

the host church who admitted to being victims of domestic violence did not participate or show any interest in being a part of the focus group. I came to realize that everyone that has survived domestic violence is not ready to do the work that is necessary for healing.

On the other hand, the two focus group participants from the host church are two different persons than those previously identified. This led me to surmise that there are many more within the host church who did not come forward. I question, in offering the space and allocating the time for session, what will drive survivors of domestic violence to the sessions to begin their healing?

I have risen to the occasion of addressing the aftereffects of domestic violence in the local church. My research and analysis shows that there is a connection between sharing one's story of abuse in a nonjudgmental church setting to the degree of guilt and shame experienced at the onset and at the end of the sessions. The research substantiates my beliefs that the church is an appropriate place for addressing the relevant issues of guilt and shame associated with domestic violence.

Where do we go from here? The church where I pastor is just one of the many churches that need to establish ministries within for domestic violence survivors. The ministry of meeting in focus group to address the aftereffects of guilt and shame must be continued. The next phase will be addressed in my final chapter of reflection, summary and conclusion.

6 REFLECTIONS, SUMMARY AND CONCLUSION

I began this research exploring the fact that survivors of domestic violence leave abusive relationships with some degree of guilt and shame. Similarly, many of the survivors of domestic violence are faithful parishioners each week in some place of worship. While many of the survivors of domestic violence are parishioners in many different churches, mosques or synagogues, their issue – the aftereffects of guilt and shame associated with domestic violence – is rarely addressed in their local place of worship. I further posited that the church's failure to address domestic violence and the aftereffects of guilt and shame is an injustice. Thus, I contend that a model of utilizing liberation, feminist and womanist theologies in the context of the local church can change how survivors of domestic violence view themselves. Liberation theology speaks to changing things in society so that the conditions can be more humane and just with a core focus on males, racism, and poverty. Feminist theology speaks to the needs of women – however, mostly European and white women. Still, womanist theology speaks to the liberation of all humankind. Of particular concern is the need to use these theological lenses of liberation, feminist and womanist theologies to develop models of ministry within the local church for survivors of domestic violence. Thus, I am indicting the church for its failure to provide social justice ministry to survivors of domestic violence. We must name, challenge, and change the way churches develop ministries to ensure that the ministries are relevant for all those who worship within and for those who will later become a part of the church community. The model that was developed accomplishes that. While the church must also address the needs of both the abused and the abuser, this research was specifically focused on the guilt and shame experienced as a result of surviving domestic violence for African American women.

In Chapter One, I shared my personal story of being abused and how it impacted this ministry. Knowing firsthand the detriment of not addressing guilt and shame as a result of surviving domestic violence and its effect on making coherent decisions speaks greatly to the need of pastors and churches to speak up against domestic violence. I share how failure to address my issues of guilt and shame as a result of surviving domestic violence left me with feelings of being flawed, unlovable, and undeserving of real love. As a means of pedagogy, sermons and workshops should be preached and conducted in the local church for continuous support to survivors of domestic violence.

One might question the need for continuous focus group ministry or whether a one-time healing service can eradicate the guilt and shame associated with domestic violence. I disagree with a one-time healing service changing the degree of guilt and shame experienced as a result of surviving domestic violence. The truth is that a one-time healing service is not sufficient to adequately heal. While healing may be initiated, I posit that there must be follow-up that comes through articulation and storytelling in a shared community. I have always believed that healing is an ongoing process.

Personally, I was affected by this project in that I became a stronger, more confident person. I, too, am not the same as I was prior to facilitating six sessions of focus group with African American women survivors of domestic violence experiencing the aftereffects of guilt and shame. While this model's demographics included only African American women survivors of domestic violence, male survivors, as well as other ethnic groups, can also benefit from this model. For male survivors of domestic violence, especially, I recommend this model along with utilizing Howard Fradkin's book, *Joining Forces: Empowering Male Survivors to Thrive*. This text is particularly suited to address the specific needs of men as they emerge as victors from incidences of domestic violence. For me, ministry is, simply, service to others. Thus, as a servant, it was rewarding to meet survivors of domestic violence where they were in their degree of guilt and shame with the intentions of not leaving them like I found them.

Further, my research documents that the aftereffects of guilt and shame associated with surviving domestic violence cannot be healed in isolation. The healing requires the support of outside sources. Outside sources can vary, but this research shows that one outside source is vital to the healing process: focus group with peers.

One of the many challenges for birthing new ministries is the follow-up and continuation of that ministry. Focus group support ministry for survivors of domestic violence experiencing guilt and shame as a result of being abused was birthed out of my own experience. I strongly believe that God called me to help women realize their self-worth, to realize that they are created in the image of God and that they are fearfully and wonderfully made. I believe that God called me to help survivors of domestic violence to transform and thrive. Unfortunately, not all pastors have the same passion. Continuation of this vital ministry will not occur until all pastors take seriously the need for the ministry and all churches come out of denial that domestic violence and its aftereffects are issues that need addressing. Additionally, I submit that church lay leaders must be empowered to realize the need for domestic violence ministry in the local church and trained to facilitate this ministry even in the wake of a new pastor, especially in those denominations who utilized itinerant ministers. This would certainly be a way of ensuring continuity of the ministry.

For this project, the biggest issue amongst the participants was blaming themselves for the abuse. While this project addressed the aftereffects of guilt and shame associated with surviving domestic violence, going forward I would have a forgiveness ritual whereby the participants can forgive themselves for legitimate issues. For example, I am aware that there are things that people are guilty of that is not related to domestic violence or surviving domestic violence. It would be important to add a ceremony on releasing guilt for the legitimate things that survivors have done that is non-domestic violence related.

As another means of fine-tuning the model, going forward I would also conduct the same stone ritual used in Session One again in Session Six to see if there was a change in the selection of colored stones which was indicative of how the survivors were feeling personally at the conclusion of the sessions. Further, I recommend that the timing and intervals between focus group sessions are consistent and equal. Timing and intervals may be contributors to why focus group participants do not continue the project. There was a variation of intervals between sessions, ranging from one week to three weeks. This may have contributed to two of the participants not continuing in the focus group. Finally, I recommend that there be preaching, teaching, and workshops on guilt and shame as a means of opening the way for those suffering with the aftereffects of guilt and shame that might be in denial. By hearing sermons, lessons or participating in workshops prior to participating in focus groups, survivors may be more open to participating in focus group sessions where the real work of confronting the aftereffects of guilt and shame really occurs.

God is placing me in positions to be a voice that will cry out against the injustice of not addressing domestic violence and bring to the forefront the aftereffects of guilt and shame as a result of surviving domestic violence, while simultaneously allowing me to reiterate the role that the church must play in doing so.

The Prophet Micah offers this challenge: "He has told you, O mortal, what is good; and what does the Lord require of you but to do justice, and to love kindness, and to walk humbly with your God?"[113] This requirement (to do justice toward others) certainly takes into account doing justice to persons who are survivors of domestic violence and who, as a result, suffer the aftereffects of guilt and shame. Like the Prophet Micah, pastors (as leaders) must take on the responsibility to lead congregations into this ministry of doing justice. As God's representatives, for the love of justice we must embrace the opportunity to do justice. The church must be the

---

[113] Micah 6:8 (New Revised Standard Version)

church; thus, both clergy and lay must commit to loving actions and courageous faith in providing support ministry for survivors of domestic violence. May all pastors, then, heed God's requirement of providing justice to survivors of domestic violence by addressing the issue of guilt and shame in the local church. After all, when all pastors believe, as I do, that engaging in this ministry is doing justice, that engaging in this ministry is what the Lord requires, then – and only then – will the pastors and churches leave an impact that is felt long after the songs are sung and sermons are preached.

Then the broken pieces can be made whole.

ABOUT THE AUTHOR

Dr. Carolyn C. Carlisle is a Budget Analyst and serves as the Lead Pastor of Rocksolid Ministries, Inc., in Columbus, Georgia. She is a gifted speaker, sought after Conference Speaker, Revival Preacher, and Workshop Facilitator. She is the Chief Executive Officer and Founder of Survivors4Survivors, Inc., a non-profit organization that advocates against domestic violence. For more information about Dr. C., please visit www.survivors4survivors.org.

APPENDICES

PARTICIPANT PRE-POST TEST CONTINUUM

Guilt   Shame

Guilt	Shame
☐ 10	☐ 10
☐ 9	☐ 9
☐ 8	☐ 8
☐ 7	☐ 7
☐ 6	☐ 6
☐ 5	☐ 5
☐ 4	☐ 4
☐ 3	☐ 3
☐ 2	☐ 2
☐ 1	☐ 1
☐ HEALED	☐ HEALED

Instructions
1. Each number represents a level of guilt (left hand side) and shame (right hand side).
2. Check the appropriate box that indicates your level of Guilt (left hand side) and Shame (right hand side).
3. Below number one represents no Guilt (left hand side) and/or no Shame (right hand side).
4. Indicate on the scale where your cognitive emotions of Guilt (left hand side) and Shame (right hand side) reside at this present moment.

Name_____ Number _____

Number	Affect
Below 1	Healed
1-3	Mild
4-6	Moderate
7-10	Severe

Session 1 Format

1. Purpose of Group
     a. Prayer
     b. Welcome
     c. Purpose of Group
     d. Dissemination of Folders and Discussion of Contents
2. Completion of Forms
     a. Confidentiality Agreement
     b. Demographics Questionnaire
     c. Pre-test
3. Introduction of Group members
     a. Who are you? Introductions utilizing the first letter of your first name and last letter of your last name to describe yourself.
     b. How are you feeling? Utilize color stones to indicate feelings.
     c. Why are you here? (3-4 sentences)

4. Soft Music
5. Closing

Session 2 Format

1. Introduction of Facilitator and Group Members
    a. Prayer
    b. Welcome
    c. Purpose of Group
    d. Dissemination of Folders and Discussion of Contents
2. Give topic of today's session (Guilt) 30 minutes
    a. Define guilt
    b. Writing in journals – Question of the day – Why do I feel guilty about the domestic violence I experienced when I did nothing wrong?
    c. Sharing
3. Break (10 minutes) Soft Music
4. Working through the guilt I feel from the abuse I received (20 minutes)
    a. Examining how we misplace the blame "If I had only done or not done this or that"
    b. Rejecting the blame and transferring it to appropriate place. Abuse is never justified.
5. Writing in journals (20 minutes)
    a. I acknowledge that the abuse was not my fault.
    b. I should not feel guilty because...
    c. In order to move forward, I need...
    d. Sharing
6. Break (10 minutes) Soft music
7. Closing
    a. Psalm 9:9-10 "The Lord is a refuge for the oppressed, a stronghold in times of trouble. Those who know your name will trust in you, for you, Lord, have never forsaken those who seek you."
    b. Closing Prayer

Session 3 Format

1. Introduction of Facilitator and Group Members (10 Minutes)
   a. Prayer
   b. Welcome
   c. Purpose of Group
   d. Dissemination of Folders and Discussion of Contents
2. Give topic of today's session (Shame) (50 minutes)
   a. Define Shame
   b. Write in journals
      1) Do you feel shamed about what happened to you?
      2) Have you ever experienced: Isolation? Felt all alone? Low Self-Esteem? Hopeless? Unworthy of love?
      3) In your experience(s) of feeling shame, did you feel cut off from God?
3. Break (10 minutes) Soft Music
4. Activity (15 minutes)
   a. Poem – "We Wear the Mask" by Paul Lawrence Dunbar
   b. Mask Activity – Give each participant a mask. Allow each participant to focus on one incident that caused them to feel ashamed. What did you see? What did you hear? How did you feel?
   c. Sharing
5. Unmasking Shame (30 minutes)
   a. Remove mask
   b. Share your shamed experience within the group setting
   c. Write about it in your journal
   d. Speak positive affirmations about yourself to yourself. Examples: I am beautiful. I am good. I do belong. I am capable. I am lovely. I have what it takes to succeed. There is a great purpose for my life.
6. Closing (5 mnutes0
   a. Find or compose a song, dance or poem that speaks specifically to you expressing your feelings about your new self-image. Share this with someone.
   b. Closing prayer

Session 4 Format

1. Introduction of Facilitator and Group Members (15 minutes)
    a. Prayer
    b. Welcome
    c. Purpose of Group
    d. Dissemination of Folders and Discussion of Contents
2. Sharing of Stories (3 hours)
3. Musical interlude in between sharing of stories
4. Closing Prayer

Session 5 Format

1. Introduction of Facilitator and Group Members (10 minutes)
   a.   Prayer
   b.   Welcome
   c.   Purpose of Group
   d.   Dissemination of Folders and Discussion of Contents
2. Give topic of today's session – "Loving the You God Created: Re-evaluating Self-Esteem" (2 hours)
   a.   Mirror exercise 1
   b.   Discovering Your God Given Worth
   c.   What is self-esteem?
   d.   Controlling your self-talk
   e.   Mirror exercise 2
3. Break (10 minutes)
4. Closing (10 minutes)
   a.   Testimonies
   b.   Recital of Poem, "Our Deepest Fear"
   c.   Prayer

Our Deepest Fear, by President Nelson Mandela, 1994 Inaugural Speech

Session 6 Format

1. Introduction of Facilitator and Group Members (10 Minutes)
   a. Prayer
   b. Welcome

2. Post-test

3. Evaluation of Sessions

4. Testimonies

5. Mary Kay Facials

6. Expressions of Gratitude

7. Closing Prayer

Sessions Evaluation

1. Were these sessions beneficial to you?   ___ Yes   ___ No

Explain_____

_____

_____

2. What was the strength of the sessions? _____

_____

_____

3. What was the weakness of the sessions? _____

_____

_____

4. Were the presenters knowledgeable of the subject? ___ Yes __No

5. Would you be willing to participate continuously in a peer focus group in the local church? ___ Yes ___ No Why or why not? _____

_____

_____

_____

6. Additional comments (Use back of page, if necessary)

_____

_____

_____

_____

Demographic Questions

Name _____ Number _____

Circle the appropriate answer to each question.

What is your age group?
18-35
36-46
47-57
58+

Are you currently?
Single
Married
Separated
Divorced
Widowed
Other

Do you have any children? Yes   No   Number of children _____

Employment Status
Unemployed
Employed   Full time   Part-time

Highest Level of Education
GED
High School
Associate Degree
College Degree
Master's Degree
Graduate Degree

Confidentiality Agreement

I, _____, do thereby promise that

I will not discuss anything that is shared in this focus group with anyone

else. All information provided is this focus group will be held in confidence

by me. Information disclosed during these sessions is not to be disclosed

or shared with anyone. Everything share within the confines of this focus

group will remain in this group.

_____

Print Name

_____

Signature

_____

Date

Bibliography

Ali-Dinar, Ali. *Letter from the Birmingham Jail [King, Jr.}*. December 30, 2013. http://www.africa.upenn.edu/Articles_Gen/Letter_Birmingham.html/ (accessed December 30, 2013).

Bancroft, Lundy. *Why Does He Do That? Inside the Minds of Angry and Controlling Men.* New York, NY: Berkley Books, 2002.

Bradshaw, John. *Healing the Shame That Binds You*. Edited by Expanded ed. Deerfield Beach, FL: HCI, 2005.

Buxton, Rod. "Domestic Violenc the church: there is an elephant in the sanctuary and no-one is talking about it -the results of a Manitoba survey." *Didaskaliia Otterburne, Man,* May 2, 2014: 51-75.

Carter, Jimmy. *A Call to Action: Women, Religion, Violence, and Power.* New York, NY: Simon & Schuster, 2014.

Clark, Ron. *Setting the Captives Free: A Christian Theology for Domestic Violence.* Eugene, OR: Cascade Books, 2005.

Colbert, Ty C. *Why Do I Feel Guilty When I've Done Nothing Wrong?* Nashville, TN: Thomas Nelson, Inc., 1993.

Cone, James. *A Bleak Theology of Liberation.* 40th. Maryknoll, NY: Orbis Books, 1997.

Cooper-White, Pamela. *The Cry of Tamar: Violence Against Women and the Church's Response.* 2nd . Minneapolis, MN: Fortress Press, 2012.

Craddock, Fred B. *Interpretation Luke: A Bible Commentary for Teaching and Preaching.* Louisville, KY: John Knox Press, 1990.

Davis, Edward Smith, interview by Carolyn Carlisle. *Ethical and Biblical Engagement for Social and Moral Imperatives: The Trials and Joys, the Ins and Outs of Being a Conference Minister with its Ddiversity* (December 9, 2014).

Davis, Sharon Ellis. *Battered African American Women: A Study of Gender Entrapment.* Lewiston, NY: Edwin Mellin Press, 2014.

Dobash, Emerald R. Dobash and Russell P. *Women, Violence, & Social Change.* New York, NY: Routledge, 1994.

Evans, Adrian C. "Loving the You God Created." *Loving the You God Created.* Mobile, AL: Adrian C. Evans, 12 10, 2014.

Fable, Jan. *"Shame".* December 29, 2013. http://www.forehealing.org/shame.html (accessed December 29, 2013).

Fluker, Walter Earl. "Black History Lecture." *McCormick Theological Seminary.* Chicago: McCormick Theological Seminary, 2014.

Fortune, Marie. *Faith Trust Institute.* September 28, 2014. http://www.faithtrustinstitute.org/blog (accessed September 28, 2014).

Fortune, Marie M. *Is Nothing Sacred? The Story of a Pastor, the Women He Sexually Abused and the Congregation He Nearly Destroyed.* Eugene, OR: Wipf & Stock Publication, 2008.

Fradkin, Howard. *Joining Forces: Empowering Male Survivors to Thrive.* Carlsbad, CA: Hay House, 2012.

Frederick, Marla F. *Between Sundays: Black Women and Everyday Struggles of Faith.* Berkeley, CA: University of California Press, 2003.

Grant, Jacquelyn. "Womanist Theology in North America." *Journal of the Interdenominational Theological Center* 16, no. 1-2 (1988-1989): 285.

Gutierrez, Gustavo. *A Theology of Liberation: History, Plitics, and Salvation.* Edited by Sister Caridad Inda and John Eagleson. Maryknoll, NY: Orbis Books, 1988.

Heath, Chip Heath and Dan. *Decisive: How to Make Better Choices in Life and Work.* New York, NY: Crown Business, 2013.

Hock, Meg Kennedy Dugan and Roger R. *It's My Life NowL Starting Over*

After an Abusive Relationship or Domestic Violence. 2nd. New York, NY: Routledge, 2006.

Hollies, Linda H. *Innter Healing for Brokwn Vessels: A Domestic Violence Survival Guide.* Cleveland, OH: The Pilgrim Press, 2006.

Hooks, Bell. *Sisters of the Yam: Black Women and Self-Recovery.* Cambridge, MA: South End Press, 2005.

Jeanne Stevenson-Moessner, Teresa Snorton, and editors, ed. *Women Out of Order: Risking Change and Creating Care in a Multicultural World.* Minneapolis, MN: Fortress Press, 2010.

Justes, Emma J. *Please Don't Tell: What to Do with the Secrets People Share.* Nashville, TN: Abingdon Press, 2014.

Kaufman, Gershen. *The Psychology of Shame: Theory and Treatment of Shame Based Syndromes.* New York, NY: Springer Publishings Company, 1996.

Kirk-Duggan, Cheryl A. *A Misbegotten Anguish: a Theology and Ethics of Violence.* St. Louis, MO: Chalice Press, 2001.

—. *A Violence and Theology.* Nashville, TN: Abingdon Press, 2006.

Knowles, Andrew. *The Bible Guide.* 1st Augsburg books ed. Minneapolis, MN: Augsburg Books, 2001.

MacArthur, John. *The MacArthur Bible Commentary: Unleashing God's Trugh, One Verse at a Time.* Nashville, TN: Thomas Nelson, 2005.

McCrary, Carolyn Akua L. "Intimate Violence Against Black Women and Internalized Shame: A Womanist Pastoral Counseling Perspective." *Journal of The Interdenominational Theological Center,* 2001.

Miles, Al. *Domestic Violence: What Every Pastor Needs to Know.* Minneapolis, MN: Fortress Press, 2000.

National Coalition Against Domestic Violence. *National Coalition Against Domestic Violence.* September 11, 2014. http://www.ncadv.org/ (accessed September 11, 2014).

Nolland, John. *Word Biblical Commentary*. Vol. 35a. Dallas, TX: Thomas Nelson, 1989.

Nouwen, Henri J M. *Making All Things New: an Invitation to the Spiritual Life*. San Francisco, CA: HarperOne, 2009.

—. *The Wounded Healer: Ministry in Contemporary Society*. New York, NY: Image Books, 1979.

Ore Lee Spragin, Jr. *Commentary on the Gospel of Luke*. n.p: CreateSpace Independent Publishing Platform, 2011.

Park, Andrew Sung. *From Hurt to Healing: a Theology of the Wounded*. Nashville, TN: Abingdon Press, 2004.

Poling, Nancy Werking. *Victim to Survivor: Women Recovering from Clergy Sexual Abuse*. Eugene, OR: Wipf & Stock Publishers, 2009.

Potter-Efron, Ronald Potter-Efron and Patricia. *Letting Go of Shame: Understanding How Shame Affects Your Life*. New York, NY: Routledge, 1989.

Stanton, Elizabeth Cady. *The Woman's Bible: a Classic Feminist Perspective*. Mineola, NY: Dover Publications, 2003.

Tatum, Scott L. *The Teacher's Bible Commentary*. Edited by Franklin H. Paschall and Herschel H. Hobbs. Nashville, TN: Broadman and Holman Publishers, n.d.

Townes, Emilie M. *Breaking the Fine Rain of Death: African-American Health Issues and a Womanist Ethic of Care*. New York, NY: Continuum, 2001.

Tracey, Steven R. *Mending the Soul*. April 2007. http://www.mendingthesoul.org/2007/04/clergy-responses-to-domestic-violence/ (accessed May 18, 2013).

Trible, Phyllis. *Texts of Terror: Literary-Feminist Readings of Biblical Narrative*. Philadelphia, PA: Fortress Press, 1984.

Weems, Renita J. *Battered Love: Marriage, Sex, and Violence in the Hebrew*

Prophet. Minneapolis, MN: Fortress Press, 1995.

Williams, Delores. *Sisters in the Wilderness.* Maryknoll, NY: Orbis Books, 1999.

Wimberly, Edward P. *African American Pastoral Care.* rev ed. Nashville, TN: Abingdon Press, 2008.

Youngblood, Robert F. *Nelson's New Illustrated Bible Dictionary.* Nashville, TN: Thomas Nelson Publishers, 1995.

Made in the USA
Columbia, SC
20 February 2023

12630363R00041